"Heather's compassionate heart and vulnerability as she shares her stories are inspirational in *All the Wild Pearls*. Beyond being a manual for sharing redemptive moments, this is a testament to the incredible power that lies in bringing our "pearls" to the light and stepping into our worth as perfectly imperfect children of God."

—**JESSICA HONEGGER**, Founder and co-CEO of Noonday Collection, Author of *An Imperfect Courage*

"*All the Wild Pearls* invites you to remember your own redemptive story. Heather vulnerably shares from her rugged journey toward redemption, beautifully comparing it to the making of a pearl. This is a gift from one woman's heart to another!"

—**ALICE FREDRICKS**, Staff Member for CRU since 1965, mentoring women around the world

"*All the Wild Pearls* is loaded with Gospel hope, from start to finish. Using an unlikely agent of change (an oyster), Heather weaves Gospel themes in a beautiful way. No matter how well you know your own redemption story (or don't), this book is both relatable and inspiring. Those who read it will benefit greatly, as Heather artfully guides readers how to capture and share their own stories – their *pearls*."

—**MATT MURPHY**, Lead Pastor, Grace Fellowship Church, Johnson City, Tennessee

"I have always loved pearls. My first pearl was a ring that I got in high school. Years later, my husband bought a beautiful strand of pearls which I continue to treasure to this day. Until I read this book though, I was unaware of the story behind a pearl! Heather displays God's beauty of grace and redemption through her own redemptive stories...her *pearls*. The bold way she shares Christ leaves me wanting to seek God's Word and presence more in my life. Heather is also my dear friend and one of the most 'salty – godly' women I know. Redemption, pearls, her story, my story, *your* story is waiting for you in this book."

—**SHERRY P. MARION**, co-founder of Rise Up! Mentoring

"Heather shares her heart with honesty and conviction in *All the Wild Pearls*. This book is not a memoir but rather a working manual for Christian women who are yet unformed; unsure that their own story has such immense value. It is not enough to know the Gospel but to know how to look deeply and then live it out uniquely. Heather uses the imagery of the pearl to coach any brave reader to grow in understanding what a treasure she is."

—**MARY BARTON NEES**, MFA, Artist, Instructor and Author of
Markers—Key Themes for Soul Survival

"Ever since the garden women have too often struggled with shame, but God sent His son Jesus so that through Him our guilt and shame would be redeemed. In *All the Wild Pearls*, Heather invites us on a journey where a life of hurt and pain is transformed into something beautiful & purposeful. This book offers women hope of redemption and the potential to see pearls come from their pain. This book also encourages and empowers women to not only write their redemption story, but to share it with others. In our generation we need hope of pearls and this book gives it to us!"

—**AMIE SPANO**, wife of Florida Rep. Ross Spano, Chairman of
the Florida Human Trafficking Working Group

"Heather is one of those storytellers who puts you on the edge of your seat, hanging onto every word. Her witty and conversational style will feel like having coffee with a dear friend. In *All the Wild Pearls*, she passionately and vulnerably depicts God's weaving of joy and pain together to bring about an exquisite piece of beauty. There is courage and healing on every page, and it will leave you inspired to write your own redemption narrative."

—**CARA TRANTHAM**, freelance writer for *Be Still Magazine* and
blogger at www.caractrantham.wordpress.com

all The wild pearls

Heather DeJesus Yates

Newberry, FL 32669

Bridge-Logos
Newberry, FL 32669

All The Wild Pearls: A Guide for Passing Down Redemptive Stories
by Heather DeJesus Yates

Copyright © 2018 by Bridge-Logos

Revised First Edition

Printed in the United States of America.

Library of Congress Catalog Card Number: 2018931854

International Standard Book Number: 978-1-61036-991-6

Editing services by ChristianEditingServices.com

Cover design: Summit Marketing | thesummitmarketing.com
and Kent Jensen | knail.com

Interior design: Kent Jensen | knail.com

Back cover bio photo: Kadees Approach Photography

Scripture taken from the New King James Version®. Copyright © 1982 by Thomas Nelson. Used by permission. All rights reserved.

Dedication

For my daughter

Your lovely name means dark-haired beauty
free from oppression. Beautiful one, no other name could
fit you any better!

May you know in the depths of your heart that out of all the
treasures God has redeemed for me—from all the pain in all my
stories—you, my darling daughter, are by far my grandest gift.

Acknowledgements

"You split the sea
So I could walk right through it
My fears were drowned in perfect love
You rescued me
And I will stand and sing
I am the child of God."

—*NO LONGER SLAVES*, BETHEL MUSIC

I owe an enormous debt of gratitude to so many people who together made this book possible. While this is simply an acknowledgement of their lives touching mine, my appreciation will continue to run deeper than I'll ever be able to put into words, but here is my attempt to start:

To Suzi—you became a friend nearly 20 years ago and then by the mysterious will of God you became my publisher! You will never fully know the impact your invitation has had on my whole family, truly you have been part of a sea-splitting wonder for us. Thank you for opening a door and allowing for what seemed impossible to become possible.

To my editor Ed—and my other happy editors Matt, Mary, Pam and Sarah, who weeded and tended diligently through these pages to keep the message and my voice clear! Your attention to detail and doctrinal wisdom have worked together to refine this work I believe will bring hope to many, just as your friendship has brought hope to me. Thank you for your expertise and generous help!

To the brave souls who not only read this book, they put their names on it! To Jessica, Matt, Amie, Mary, Alice, Sherry and Cara, I thank you for your kind words and pray this book lives up to them!

Jessica Honegger—your own courage to write your story continued to spur my own work along, thank you for your big "yes" to be a part of this project and for relentlessly partnering in God's dream of building a flourishing world!

To Kent at Bridge Logos and Rick and the team at Summit Marketing for all your help in displaying the message in this book in so many lovely ways. You all put the icing on the cake and it makes this girl's soul rejoice!

To the Staff at Doe River Gorge who create space for people to commune with God—and especially for Hannah and Clif who let me take a deep pause in their home so I could hear God give me a new song, thank you!

To hands down the best book club on the planet—Allison, Robyn, Angela, Amy, Lauren, Sarah and both Jennifer's—your cheer-leading, empathy, willingness to read and discuss this book in its rough stages, sending all the texts with all the hearts and giving all the hugs has deepened me in God's love. Thank you, girls!

For my friend and often counselor—Michele, you spoke truth to my soul and told me when it was time to write again. Your empathy and wisdom helped me break out of hiding into marvelous light and your words that launched me will stay with me for a lifetime: "Heather, don't overthink this, just enjoy the process!" May I continue learning to live in the way of joy.

To the coffeehouses that kept me caffeinated and comforted for the long journey: Open Doors Coffeehouse brewing espresso and stirring up hope for tomorrow's leaders by supporting local mentoring ministry, thank you! Also, the friendly staff at the Pinnacle Starbucks who welcomed me often with, "Heather who is writing a book!" You gave life with that greeting, thank you!

To my community of "Mama Bears"—you read my words on the blog and give me such encouragement to keep resting in the love of God and showing up with my voice, I am so grateful for you! Special thanks to Cheryl, "Mama Joan", Lois, Melanie and my dear friend Malia who have helped me stay the course—you've sent the texts, celebrated the milestones, and have prayed the prayers along the way. I treasure you as some of the finest gifts a girl can receive and thank you!

To a special friend who has served as a doula for this book –Jennifer C., you have been a sister and encourager from the start, even celebrating the contract for this book that came on your own birthday! For the daily texts, words filled with courage, reminders to write and for being on my side every step of the way, I cannot thank you enough!

To Elizabeth and the loyal band of "quiet retreaters" who have faithfully nudged me back to solitude and silence with God for my strength and formation, thank you! Elizabeth, your kind friendship and soul-coaching all these years has helped me root deep in the safety and security of God's love, may you be blessed in all you do.

To Emily P. Freeman and the Hope*writers community—your faithfulness to share what you are learning with other artists has helped steer my own journey of sharing life-giving messages with my voice. Thank you for helping me form and release my "art" in the writing of this book!

To Allie, our beautiful, talented and tender-hearted college girl who has partnered with us in loving our daughter—especially on Friday afternoons so I could write this book! We love you and are so proud of the woman you are and are becoming. I wrote this with your future faith journey in mind, so may you collect your own wild pearls and pass them down as you live your life out fully loved! The University of Tennessee will never be the same!

To my Dad—your wish for me to share my story (no matter how it reflected upon you) so that others can hear about Jesus' love and redemption plan for us has maybe been your most precious gift to me. Thank you for modeling humility for me and for stirring up my faith that resurrection life is possible for each of us.

To my Mom—who pioneered a faith path her children and grandchildren could follow, a path you continue to plow today. I admire you and am the woman I am today in large part because of the God you pointed me to in your own redemptive stories. Thank you for sharing your life with me and giving me permission to share it in these pages, you brave and dear woman!

To each person who picks up this book and reads through the pages of my story, thank you. May you receive the hope of the Gospel and discover and record your own redemption stories! May you grow in confidence sharing your stories with others declaring how God has worked in your life!

To Jonathan, a.k.a. Grizz, I have saved you for the end because I knew I'd need to wait for the tears to clear out. I really don't know where to begin. If you had not pursued me, if you had not believed in me, if you had not nudged me back to myself with Jesus thousands of times, this book would not be here today. For all your white t-shirts you let me cry all my make-up on, and for all the times you reminded me why I need to show up to my life, and for all the times you sincerely asked, "what can I do for you?"—thank you. Our daughter has her Mommy's redemption story written here thanks to her Daddy.

And to the One without whom I'd have nothing to say: God, may every second and every word be lifted up to You now as an offering of gratitude for all the wonderful ways you have already brought joy and continue still to redeem all my wild pain into pearls.

—Heather DeJesus Yates

Table of Contents

an Introduction

Pearls are the product of pain.
For some unknown reason, the shell of the oyster
gets pierced and an alien substance—a grain of sand—slips
inside. On the entry of that foreign irritant, all the resources
within the tiny, sensitive oyster rush to the spot and begin
to release healing fluids that otherwise would have remained
dormant. By and by the irritant is covered and the wound is
healed—by a pearl. No other gem has so fascinating a history.
It is the symbol of stress—a healed wound...a precious, tiny
jewel conceived through irritation, born of adversity, nursed
by adjustments. Had there been no wounding, no irritating
interruption, there could have been no pearl.[1]

We all have a story to tell. Even if you don't write a book, your story is worth telling.

As women who have put our trust in Jesus Christ to forgive us our sins, we have a redemption story. We can tell a story of what led us to one moment of faith when our wounded old nature was crucified with Jesus and born in our spirit was a new perfect nature—Christ in us. Our wounds were healed and something precious formed in us—like a pearl! For some of us this moment of change pierced through a wild struggle of belief and circumstances, while for others it rolled over the heart like a gentle ripple on a calm sea. No matter the events surrounding our redemption story, it is the Story contained within our stories—the Gospel—that give our stories transformational power.

But why stories, or to use a term used in Scripture, testimonies?

It sounds shocking to state it this way, but Jesus did not commission the disciples of the early Church to go be good people, or to go serve others selflessly, or even alleviate poverty. Certainly, the love they were shown by God inspired them to love others in practical ways, and God teaches us to obey Him by loving others. But this is not how Jesus framed their mission.

Jesus launched them out to simply *be His witnesses*.

To be a witness is to testify by personal account. Jesus commissioned the first disciples, and those of us who follow Him today, to be His witnesses, or go tell our redemptive stories to the uttermost parts of the earth. When we do, we can expect the Gospel to do what only it can do: a hidden work of multiplicity in the hearts of hearers. Without really understanding our role we change our world by passing down our redemptive stories.

But the power is not in our good storytelling, it is in the good Story we tell.

A redemptive story is not like any other story because it hinges upon the Gospel's work in our brokenness of soul, bringing us always closer to the beautiful hope of redemption. Wherever we have wounds, we find healing met in Christ and the result is a new redemptive story. In fact, we have lots of stories of the Gospel's work in our lives. We can tell of the daily ways Jesus' presence with us wraps our distressed souls with comfort, strengthens us to endure suffering, and reshapes pain into priceless character.

Simply put, a redemptive story is a story of a healed wound.

A pearl.

The beauty and worth of pearls has been revered since antiquity. Women have long held a tradition of passing down precious heirlooms to the next generation of women in their families, or to beloved friends. This impartation of beauty and story speaks to the presence of God among us, drawing us to treasure what truly holds meaning, and to share it so our influence stretches beyond our brief life. It is not out of rule or regulation that we pass down strands of pearls, but out of a love for others to have what we have, to learn what we have learned, and to enjoy what we have enjoyed. So too may this book help women in our generation recognize the beauty and worth of our redemptive stories and be stirred up in love to pass them down to our next generation. As women, we can choose to heed the firm nudge from Titus in Scripture to be intentional with our time by investing it in the women growing around us. We can choose to see our place in history and accept the challenges as uniquely ours. We can encourage one another with hope that our lives matter, and that God can use us and our redemptive stories to bear new life.

But not all women are telling their story.

Perhaps some women believe their story is too simple to share because they put their trust in Christ at a young age. Maybe some still carry shame connected to their story and are holding back out of fear of what others may think about them. Others may want to share their stories but believe they aren't good enough at writing or speaking to share them with confidence or don't think they matter to anyone.

When I was on staff as women's ministry leader at my church, one of my roles was to do baptism interviews. I loved hearing the stories of women encountering Jesus, hearing the Gospel and responding to it with faith and joy. But what I noticed over the years was that in almost every conversation, no matter how long the woman walked with Christ, she still lacked a degree of confidence in restating her personal redemption story.

I was surprised and saddened by this pattern and wondered how many other women simply lacked confidence in telling their redemption story? I wondered too how many women are sitting on meaningful redemptive stories where Christ has met them in heartache or hardship, rescuing them with hope even long after salvation. Maybe they were listening to shame and discounting that they had anything to offer, or were afraid of rejection and being judged, or just didn't know how to put those stories into words either.

In the baptism interviews, our first commitment was to keep the Gospel clear, and the second commitment was to make sure the congregant understood how the Gospel and her faith worked together, and in her own words. Through the course of a meeting or two, and an exchange of emails, we would work together until she had her testimony, or redemption story, clarified in just a handful of sentences that could be read in under 2 minutes. Several times I had the privilege of being in the physical presence of the woman as she distilled her statement. Witnessing her joy over capturing her own story was so satisfying! You could almost see her soul fill with power, her shoulders would open wide as she relaxed and stabilized herself on new ground, firmly equipped with a testimony of her own. I wanted to see more women experience this kind of empowerment in owning their stories!

This is where you come in friend, I want you empowered to own your redemption and redemptive stories too!

Each of us holds within our lives a collection of stories that follow a recurring pattern of unexpected pain, a revelation of God's presence, a process of healing, and ultimately a priceless purpose. But not all of us have unearthed these stories, practiced sharing them or at least we have not written them down for the encouragement of others in our lives.

This book is written to help you write what most needs to be written.

To accomplish this goal though, we are going to take a little journey. This book is, in part, the memoir of an ordinary little oyster. You heard me right. She will be a kind guide, a little friend I've affectionately named "Wild Pearl" for the purposes of connecting better with her story. In each chapter you will first hear a little from her story, in her own words, and as the chapters unfold, so will her story.

But this book is also my own redemption story, along with some other redemptive stories I've collected over my now 40 years. In each chapter you will hear me share some of my own stories, and my redemption story that steadily unfolds along with Wild Pearl's. Told together, we hope our stories of where we came from, how we came to be, what happened to us that shaped us, and what God did to redeem our pain, will help you discover yours.

I have to say, I have learned a lot about oysters by writing this book, more than I ever cared to know. Through the plight of the oyster, I have come to better recognize God's work in my own life, gain awe for the magnificent attention to detail he puts into our unique design, accept our natural and inadequate ways of self-protecting, and am even more beholden to Jesus for the incredible sacrifice He made to bring me into freedom today and eternal hope forever. It is one thing to know God adopted me as His daughter in spite of being His enemy, but it is wildly delightful to discover that He takes the backwards ways I respond to pain and transforms even my contributing mess into something priceless as well.

Now, no metaphor runs the length of the race with you to the end, I know. Ultimately oysters do not have souls, and we will need to depart from Wild Pearl at times in order to apply God's truth to us, the soul-bearers. But if you bear with me and wait for the message that runs deeper than the metaphor, I think you will be surprised by how rich God's goodness settles in even the tiniest places of His creation.

There are two kinds of stories you will capture throughout this book. One is your redemption story, how you were God's enemy and now are His beloved child. If you don't know how to confidently tell your redemption story, this book guides you and gives you the tools you need to form your story, so you can share it with others. The other kind of story I call your redemptive stories. These are the times in your life where you were once bound in pain of some kind, but Jesus rescued you and used it to do a far greater work in your life. You may not always see the "good" in the pain yet, and we aren't going to force or fake it, but where you are discovering His sufficient grace, this book gives you the space to record it for the women who need to be strengthened, including you! If you are struggling to see hope for painful places where shame is shouting loud, may our oyster friend Wild Pearl be a reminder to us that our suffering is momentary, and our afflictions light, while an eternal weight of glory is being produced for us beyond all comparison.

Before you get started, let me tell you how to best let this book serve you. You will notice the chapters follow a sequence purposefully because they guide us progressively through the stages of a pearl's life, offering us a visual aid to better recognize the stages of a redemptive story. At the end of each chapter there are discussion questions. These questions are designed to capture your fresh response to that stage of your story, and hopefully they'll just add to the enjoyment of your journey!

Also, at the end of each of the three main sections (Formation, Retrieval and Display), there will be a space for you to capture your story up to that point. When you reach the end of the book, you will get the chance to pull it all together to shape your own unique "Pearl" so you can begin sharing its beauty with others. I hope you enjoy this process, and grow not only in understanding your own story, and the stories of others, but also that you get the opportunity to practice sharing stories among others who journey with you! After all, we are His witnesses, so let's use this time to practice!

So, if you are ready it is time to begin a journey that will guarantee your ending is done well. And speaking of endings, at the end of all the things this is what I desire: a kingdom of women and men standing before God with all our collected holy and unholy moments, and all our redemption and redemptive stories pointing to His story...because then in exchange, by His own grace, I expect He will give us *all the wild pearls*.

the Formation

the Deep

"Superficiality is the curse of our age.
The doctrine of instant satisfaction is a primary spiritual
problem. The desperate need today is not for a greater number
of intelligent people, or gifted people, but for deep people." [2]

Oysters can grow in anywhere from 8 to 120 feet deep in water, depending on the kind. In tropical regions we can be found submerged at the roots of mangrove trees, and occasionally in low tides we can become exposed. If an oyster is found open, it is dead and should not be eaten. In the 18th century, satirist Jonathan Swift is often credited with saying,

"He was a bold man that first ate an oyster."

But she was a wise woman who waited to see how the man fared first.

There are over 150 varieties of oysters harvested and sold in North America, yet they comprise a total of only 5 species of oysters. But the oysters you eat come from a different family, the Ostreidae family, while the oysters or molluscs that produce beautiful pearls come from the Aviculidae family.[3] Regardless of the breed, there is one thing all us oysters have in common. Every oyster is born in water. We grow and live in the water, and without the water, we die.

So naturally, the deep is where I start. Hi. I'm Wild Pearl, an ordinary pearl oyster of the Aviculidae family. One of thousands like me in my neighborhood. My story starts in the waters off the coastal city of Hepu, in the southern part of the Guangxi ("Gwan-see") Province of China. The water has always been home; I don't know any different really. For as far as I can see to every side there are oysters like me, doing what I'm doing, just hanging out. There is a faint hint of a light that occasionally shimmers down; I could set it to a timer if I had one. I'm drawn to this mysterious light, and though I don't know where it comes from, I just know it's different than the shadows.

For as long as I can remember, I have been deathly afraid of deep water. It's not because I'm afraid of drowning. I am a good swimmer trained by some of the finest Florida Gulf Coast waters. The Emerald Coast beaches of Destin and Sandestin offer wide stretches of shallow crystal green waters to wade in, far from deep plunges. I grew up in paradise and was spoiled by the pleasure of always seeing my feet when I swam. But it was early on that the deep became a terror for me, and not just at the beach, but in boggy bayous, lakes, even in pools.

There is one word that helps explain why I am so afraid of deep water, and I'm sure it is the same for many people, especially of my generation.

JAWS.

The classic came out a couple years before I was born but was just as terrifying a decade later when I watched the horror unfold on Amity Island for myself. I was only in elementary school but quickly became fixated on the deep. I poured over picture books with deep water creatures. I sat hypnotized whenever shows featured sea life or shipwreck. I chose the dusty tattered book on the Titanic for my 4th grade book report and read the relic cover to cover.

I was drawn to the deep, but was terrified of it too, because of what I knew lurked in the shadows.

My dad was, and still is, an avid fisherman. He could fish off a pier, shoreline, bridge, boat, jetty or anything that suspended him above water long enough to cast his rod. It would not surprise me if he had saltwater in his Puerto Rican veins, because as thin as his daddy long legs are, he is built for standing well in swell.

I didn't take to fishing like my girl cousins, much to my dad's dismay. I preferred the safety of the tri-fold lounge chair with a good book and journal, where the greatest danger was an uneven sunburn or the inevitable flesh pinch when my squishy places oozed through the cheap plastic straw weave suspending me above the sand. I tried fishing as a kid but never could quite master the coordination of it all.

Or the silence.

I fished for hats, calf muscles, wood planks, but never actually got hook to water. My only contribution to ocean-inspired meals was tossing the crab bucket. My dad even called me "Bunky" because of his pastime of crabbing while my mom was pregnant with me, or "bunking" for crabs as he would say.

Feeding me good seafood could be a love language of mine. I eat just about any fish or crustacean. And you don't have to warn me, I know the dark truth about crab and shrimp, and what they eat, but my love especially for shrimp runs deep. Dwell on the bottom you beautiful pink treasures, I don't care, I love you always.

Most of our weekends were spent at the beach, either with my dad fishing, with my grandparents, or with my family together. Sometimes, when I was in early elementary school, my dad would let me play on the shore while he walked the Destin pier to the furthest tip to fish. The thought of leaving a child alone on a public beach seems like terrible parenting to me now. My mom would have lost her mind if she knew. At the time, though, I don't remember thinking anything of it except adventure! That is, until this one day.

Dad bought me a new float. It was a long narrow yellow float, the cheap kind the color of banana with a pillow and ribbed air panels. I could hardly wait for him to finish blowing it up so I could try it out on my own. We must have had some storm weather recently, and I knew exactly where I wanted to go with my new float. There was a narrow strip of bright light green water about a third of the way out the length of the pier. Oftentimes this would indicate a sand bar, which was like discovering gold. The plan was to float out to the sand bar, stand up and then "walk on water" in front of all the tourists who didn't know the secret of the sand bar.

In my zeal, I cleared the breakers, wrangled onto my banana float, toe and hand paddled my way over the now gentle waves, and started to disembark from my float. It only took seconds before I realized I had been deceived.

Unfortunately, another secret of the sand bar is sometimes it isn't a sand bar. Sometimes it's just bright light green deep water.

Fear of the deep pinned me down onto the float as if the water formed an adhesive between my skin and the plastic. I couldn't turn my head to the left or to the right for fear of losing balance and falling in. My mind drummed up the worst. I kept my head straight and my face pointed up to the sun, eyes squinting until I reached the shadow of the pier. Then I noticed a crowd forming on the pier above me, pointing down at me. Being a little on the heavier side, my first thought was that they were being snarky about my bathing suit. Give me a break people! If only that was the case though. I started to pick up on the faint sound of my dad's voice, yelling, and as it grew louder I noticed him running toward the crowd gathering above me.

"Bunky! Stay still! Don't move!"

My mind was right, the worst was happening except I still didn't know exactly what that meant. My breathing had stopped, I was unofficially going to break the record for holding the longest breath. I wanted to scream and flail wildly, but I could see my dad's face—I knew survival called for remaining calm, and yet as paralyzed in fear as I was somehow curiosity got the better of me. I stared unblinkingly at the crowd above and my dad and watched them turn away and run to the other side of the pier, giving me the all-clear so I could peek at what had them spellbound beneath me. Still one with the float I shifted slightly to look down into the diamond studded emerald waters and took in all the information I needed with that one peek. Barely past me swimming along the surface of the earth below was an eight-foot hammerhead shark! Just the sight of it was enough to drain all the blood from my limbs. I could barely move and remember only my dad coming for me out in the deep and tugging my limp float-sealed body back to shore. It would be days before the feeling would fully return to my legs. Someone notified the authorities with fish & wildlife, the shark was tagged and sent back out to deeper waters, but in a deep sense he stayed with me forever.

"Deep calls unto deep at the noise of Your waterfalls; All Your waves and billows have gone over me."

—PSALM 42:7

Deep waters are but a shadow, like all things in our creation, of another deep. A spiritual deep, a deep I also love, and yet avoid at times too. This deep is magnificent, beautiful, can be quiet, is mysterious, and is unsearchable, though many have tried to plummet its ends. This deep is home to beautiful treasures and cliff-edge plunges that can catch my heart in my throat just like in the deep water. Sinking into this deep has frightened me at times because of what may consume me. I can imagine the worst, and I'm acutely aware of how fragile I am when I am exposed.

God is not only the creator of the deep waters, of the land, the sky and all creatures. God is Spirit, and God made all the things through His mighty spiritual power. He then allowed for the story to be recorded in the first few chapters of the book of Genesis. God was in the beginning, together with His Son and Holy Spirit, creating with words, building and forming incomprehensible beauty in perfection. He divided light from darkness, atmospheres, and land from sea. Out of nothing, an "earth without form," He made everything, and let the earth bring forth vegetation that yields seed according to its kind. God spoke the sun, the moon, and the stars into being, and let the creatures of the sea, the land and the sky take flight, all according to their kind. In the fullness of His triune nature, Father, Son, and Holy Spirit, He made a human in His own image, a soul-bearer who could think, and choose, and love.

God gave instruction to the man, and invited him into liberty so abundant, he had the run of the planet as far as the eye could see. Nothing was withheld from him to enjoy except for one simple boundary. The fruit of one tree was off limits. God made a woman for the man, out of the man, to be his ideal companion. God saw that all His creation, everything He had made, was good. They all lived peacefully, worked easily, walked together in the cool of the day in open fellowship, no guilt, no shame and no fear.

So, for a while, the deep was safe.

But jaws worse than shark teeth attacked the woman one day. The man was bitten too.

The jaws of sin closed in on humanity long before we could ever know it, in a place where the deep once held no terror or shame for us. All because of an intruder, an irritant, the enemy of God, a cunning serpent with a masterful agenda. The man and the woman belonged there, they were given the authority to rule and subdue the earth. Reign did not belong to this serpent, but soon roles would reverse. The intrusion was a deception—a deceiver spoke with the woman. The deception was the Word of God twisted, a seed thought was planted in her head that God was holding out on her, that He could not be trusted. An appeal was made to her flesh, to her eyes, to her pride, and it worked. She was deceived. She forgot the liberty and goodness of God she was given in abundance, and for a moment believed the lie that even more would be better for her. It was not enough to be made by, loved by and in easy relationship with God—she wanted to be like God.

We learn from Scripture though that the man was not deceived, he knew the command of God, so it is likely he knew what Eve's chewing of that forbidden fruit meant.[4] He had the ability to stop the progression of sin in the garden. His ability to choose was what made him God's unique creation. With his choice he could choose to love or not love God. But now his choice was one between a Rock and a woman. Scripture is silent on this point, but to resist the temptation could have meant he would have stayed in communion with his Creator but would lose fellowship with this woman. Perhaps for a split second he wondered if God could start over, make another woman? To eat though, would then mean he would keep his wife, but lose fellowship with his God. The burden, then, really all fell on his choice in a moment when I imagine all the creatures of the heavenlies held their breath.

But what Scripture is clear on is that they both chose to do the one thing God said not to do, the one thing that was restricted out of all the freedom spread wide before them. The effect of their choice: they ascended out of the protective waters of perfection and washed ashore, naked and exposed. The purity of innocent life was stripped away by the new knowledge of good and evil, and the nature of all humanity was forever changed. The fruit Adam and Eve would bear now would be according to a different kind than originally intended. A sin nature could bear only sin natures, and so this is our plight. As descendants of a fallen Adam and Eve, who bear fruit according to their kind, we are born already with a problem we cannot solve. We are born separated from God by our sin nature, and no matter how hard we try to be good nothing we do can change how we start. Indeed, all have sinned and fall short of the glory of God because of one man's sin.

God's creation in Eden for the man and the woman was like a shell with soft belly life inside, a soft and luscious life. The shell of Eden's boundaries protected the inner life from harsh elements, from a reality that it could not handle. There was danger in the deep, an evil lurked and had limited power, but entered the safety of their shell, made a cut through a lie, and a wound of shame formed instantly. In the moment they ate, their eyes opened to their nakedness. The cells in their beings reconstructed and the rot of sin began the slow decaying work in the body. Weeds began to form from sin seed now in the ground, the earth became hard and tilling would now cause strain and sweat. Making bread would now be back-breaking.

And of all the gems in Eden described, the sardius, topaz, diamond, beryl, onyx, jasper, sapphire, emerald, carbuncle, and the gold...I find it interesting that there is no mention of the pearl. But why would there be? There was no cut, no wound and so no need for healing. But on this epic day, the day the irritant in the deep slid deceitfully into the shell of the garden of God cutting His woman and His man with sin, I wonder if in this same moment in the quiet deep waters nearby a formation began in a little unsuspecting oyster. As Eve stitched her own covering for pain could it be that a newly cut oyster began her own covering work. A redemption story was now unfolding for all of creation, for in the hidden places God was taking the broken and preparing something far more beautiful. He was making way for a pearl.

MY REDEMPTION STORY

Growing up I didn't know much about God, or how the earth or people came into being. The only thing I did learn was to pray before I went to sleep: "Now I lay me down to sleep, I pray the Lord my soul to keep. If I should die, before I wake, I pray the Lord my soul to take." I heard my mom say it, so I said it, but I had no idea what I was saying. I never talked like that either, "I lay me down...". It just wasn't me. It was our way though, our habit, our tradition, and it felt good to have a routine. It comforted me to pray before I went to sleep, I liked it, but I didn't know why. I didn't know what a soul was, and for some reason never asked questions. I feared dying, every day, and it may have been the fear of dying that motivated me to pray diligently, every night. I had nightmares a lot, I was afraid of the dark as well as the deep. My dad underestimated the impact of television and images on little children and would watch scary movies with me in the room at an early age. Needless to say, I didn't sleep well, and I still struggle with nightmares sometimes.

This is just the first part of my redemption story, you will discover more as each chapter unfolds. But for now, I'll leave this part of my story with this observation I only made because this book has made me look back on my faith journey. Even that simple nightly prayer did a wonderful thing for my faith story. Acknowledging God even in that simple childhood routine helped to prepare my heart to believe in God and eventually trust in the power of His Son to save me.

Maybe I love shrimp because I too can tend to be a bottom-feeder. Even with my spirit alive because of Jesus' resurrected life in me, I still fall for the tricks of the enemy with his dangling promises of more. I can settle for impostor gods just like Eve when they appeal to the lust of my flesh, the lust of my eyes, or the pride of my heart.

I've also become quite agile at avoiding God. It is relatively easy to avoid the deep when you are swimming, just as it is relatively easy to resist being close to God. In fact, it is more challenging to enter the deep and the intimate awareness of the presence of God than it is to keep from it. As intrigued as I've been of the deep and as rooted as my relationship is with God, my life has also been marked by my creative energies spent in avoiding them both as well.

So how does one avoid the deep places with God? That part is simple.

You just become a master of staying shallow.

There are many weeks when I look back and the total number of times I tuned out in parenting, forgot I had a husband, ate and served unbalanced fast foods, gained the weight back, neglected exercise because yes, sometimes socks are just too much work, outweighs the number of successes I believe I can celebrate. In those moments, the last thing I want to do is watch a drama or suspense on television. I just watched it all week unfold in my life! I want rom coms (romantic comedies), and I want them all day long. I want a marathon of Hallmark Channel movies, Golden Girls re-runs, or feel-good movies on Netflix. Don't ask me hard questions, I don't want to see people suffering, just entertain me and let me daydream about easy, uncomplicated, predictable and scripted artificial lives where everyone smiles, hugs, holds hands or kisses at the end, but does nothing indecent because they aren't married.

Of course, we meet people in the shallow, it's not a bad place. It's a wading place, and many splash about there. It can be light and fun, and the air is easy to take in, which is why most of us stay there. It's comfortable, controllable, we can see our feet for miles. We can play in the shallow, we can recover and recreate in the shallow, we live a lot of our lives in the shallow, we buy groceries in the shallow.

But we heal in the deep, in the quiet places of the soul with God.

King David knew the comfort of being in intimate fellowship with God, where "deep calls to deep" as God's Spirit communicates with our souls. But David was human too and resisted the deep of God. We just all do it.

Even while I tried writing this chapter, I have resisted the deep places within myself and with God. So far, writing a book has meant me de-cluttering my entire clothing and accessory collection, re-ordering every space in every drawer using Marie Kondo's method.[5] If you haven't read her book "The Life-Changing Magic of Tidying Up" it's worth it even to read the plight of socks.

I've also learned how to make the world's best chocolate pudding, which touches my age-old way of resisting all the deeps: food. This particular form of resistance does not have the power over me today it has had in my past, but it's an old trick and I'm still in this body, so there you have it.

My husband thought all my cooking and cleaning this year was because of the solar eclipse, since it is so unlike me to organize my closet and cook, especially in the same year, but no.

These are just a few of the ways I wade in the shallow.

And as I have resisted, I have grown restless and dull toward God, at the same time. I have noticed myself getting more anxious, fearful and self-absorbed. I have believed an old lie that

God is angry at me, or is holding out on me, and by now I have learned to see these as signals for a starved soul. Over a month ago I began to pray about this pattern setting in, and my disinterest in reading Scripture. I prayed for a renewed desire to read, to pray, to worship, but also committed to just doing it in small ways in hope that a desire would return at some point. About a week later, during nap time one day I happened to sit in my living room to watch television for a few quiet minutes before doing the next task on my ever-growing list. I had been reading small bits of Scripture in the early mornings, not with much zeal, but it was my simple way of showing up with God. On the TV menu, I recognized the name of a Bible teacher I heard of from an older and wiser mentor friend who loves to study Scripture with this teacher. Les Feldick turned 90 this summer, is a rancher, but loves a simple study of Scripture verse-by-verse and teaches anyone who will sit still long enough to study and listen with him.[6] At the sound of his calming sage voice, and the familiar cadence of verses being read over, my soul literally felt like it was filling up. I even jumped up to run and grab my Bible and journal to take some notes, it just tasted so good to me.

The next morning the good taste of Scripture lingered in my heart, so I ran to the basement before my daughter woke up. I went to his website, and noticed that all the teachings were available, starting with Genesis 1, and began studying Scripture along with my elderly rancher friend. My hunger was nearly insatiable as I devoured teachings on Genesis and discovered new wonders from even this very familiar creation story.

God rescued me in my apathy and disinterest. He drew me back from the shallow into the deep with Him and used an elderly rancher's love for Scripture. Like a good marriage, it is encouraging to know that even after many years of living life together, we can still learn new things about this God we live with daily, and that He continues to find creative ways to woo us!

So why do we resist the deep places with God? Why do we resist being still and quiet with our souls to listen to the Creator? We resist going deep for a few reasons. For one, we may not know Him, and unless He calls us into relationship with Him, we won't go. Second, we know something is off in us, we know we fall short of perfection, so we resist being seen—by everyone. Even if we have a relationship with Jesus we can still resist being quiet with Him because we can forget what the Gospel says about us now. Much of my life is about coming back to what I most need to remember, maybe this is true for you too? We can forget that Jesus took both sin and shame. We forget there is nothing we must fix about ourselves before we can acknowledge His presence with us. We fall for the serpent's deceit and believe like Eve. We feel the effects of shame—so we hide, we distract, we search for cover, for anything to shield us from the presence of God. We blame shift, hold grudges, numb our senses, we turn up the volume in our homes, in our schedules, we labor, we toil under the sun.

We wade in the shallow.

But the Gospel tells us the hammerhead has been removed from the waters for those who trust in Jesus. There are no sharks lurking in our space with God anymore. The garden of God is safe once again, all because of what got dealt with on the cross. Yet no one will go into the depths unless she is weary of the superficial.

Are you weary yet?

The Way to Pearl[7]
To get to the happy ending that dazzles
and shimmers with all its glory, attention and
immeasurable worth—we must go back,
and not only back, but below. Way below.
For it is in the Deep where
all the greatest treasures are stored.

DISCUSSION QUESTIONS
CHAPTER 1—THE DEEP

YOUR REDEMPTION STORY

What do you remember believing about God as a child, if you thought of Him?

How did you think the earth and people came to be growing up? Were you taught how the creation account in the book of Genesis explains the beginning of all the things, or something else?

What did you learn about Adam and Eve, and the sin that changed everything? If it has changed over the years, what do you believe now?

How would you describe your childhood relationship with God?

What did you consider your "Rock" growing up, if not God? A philosophy, a thing, a person, a dream?

_____

_____

_____

OTHER REDEMPTIVE STORIES

Describe how you have resisted God at any time—how hiding out in the shallow has looked in your life.

_____

_____

_____

Describe a time God wooed you back into deeper fellowship with Him.

_____

_____

_____

2

the Cluster

"You can kiss your family and friends good-bye and put miles between you, but at the same time you carry them with you in your heart, your mind, your stomach, because you do not just live in a world but a world lives in you."

—FREDERICK BUECHNER[8]

{*Let's go back in time a bit, I would like to stretch the parameters of our little oyster friend for a moment, and imagine her parents enjoying a romantic honeymoon and a nice plankton seafood dinner before we go any further. It doesn't work this way for oysters but call me old-fashioned. Now with great joy, our little oyster is born, in the water, and for about two weeks she is but one larva among a few hundred thousand launched from her mother's fertilized eggs.*}

I was a spat, and that is that.

Yet even as a tiny one, I was responsible for my own well-being at an early age. I don't remember much, of course, but I knew I had to find somewhere to root—a reef, a cluster. I knew my survival was dependent upon me finding a safe place to land. The challenges were fierce as predators relentlessly swarmed around me. I didn't know what feeling safe meant, back then, or that I needed to feel safe, that this was even important. Looking back, I remember being an anxious little spat, feeling all taste and swallow in a shark-infested world. But I had a parent nearby, and her parent near her, so I attached to her hard rock surface and started at my own concretion work.

My shell was clustered in a small town in southern New Jersey.

Vineland.

Considering what I grew up hearing about Vineland, how my parents arrived there, and what happened there, it is ironic that I would later understand Jesus as the Vine. Jesus was never in any association I carried with Vineland.

In my childhood I received a lot of messages from my family of origin, some intended and many unintended. I established beliefs about communication, marriage, love, work, worth, beauty, and about being a family, but I didn't hear about the Bible, worship, faith, salvation, eternity, even about the Ten Commandments. I certainly didn't know anything about grace. My dad's mother attended Catholic mass, but she didn't speak English and we rarely saw her. My mom's parents went to a church on a military base for several months after both suffered a significant health scare in their 50's, but after a short while they stopped going.

My own parents had nothing to do with church, that is until my mom had a head-on confrontation with God in 1981. She was experiencing tremendous pain in her life from accumulated shame and grief and was considering how to end her pain by taking her life. What she didn't expect, though, was to see on the TV screen a man with the 700 Club[9], looking straight at her saying essentially, "You've been running all your life looking for love, while God is right there waiting to give it to you."

As a teenager, my mother turned to drugs and alcohol to numb the pain of rejection she perceived from her parents. In one season, she faced the choice between jail or rehabilitation, and chose rehab. She began a faith-based program at Teen Challenge[10] in San Antonio, Texas. One of Teen Challenge's first stories was of the ministry founder David Wilkerson's relationship with Nicky Cruz, a former teen gang member who trusted in Christ in 1958. Cruz' story was told in the book, "Run Baby Run", and was shared often with other teens in the program.[11] So my mom was well-acquainted with the metaphor of running from God when she heard the message on her television that night. She knew love was what she was always after, like all of us. There was no doubt left in her mind then when she heard the words coming from the man on the television, that God had been pursuing her heart. This time when she heard the Gospel again, my mom put her trust in Jesus Christ to forgive her of her sins, right there in our living room. She also began to recall Scriptures that had been sown into her during her time at Teen Challenge over a decade earlier. Truly, God's word planted in hearts is never wasted. The Scriptures taught to my mom accomplished the task God intended, and in this case, it was to draw my mom into a healing relationship with the only perfectly good Father.

My mom was unquestionably changed by the Gospel, but it would be a long time before she would understand just how much God loved her through that sacrifice. It would also be a winding journey through denominations and organized churches for us before we would land somewhere my mom could settle. She was alone in her faith, among all her family, but was committed to taking my brother and I with her to visit churches.

Oh, how grateful I will forever be for Teen Challenge, the 700 Club, and that surrendered and broken young woman who trusted Jesus one night on a living room floor.

"Before I formed you in the womb I knew you, before you were born, I set you apart..."

—JEREMIAH 1:5

Oysters tend to grow in clusters, one on top of the other. This cluster growing is why wild oysters tend to have "gnarly shapes" as one oyster farmer put it, instead of the nice deep cup associated with farmed oysters.[12]

No oyster chooses her shell, or cluster for that matter. She is simply formed within one. The same is true for us, and our families of origin. Long before we ever came to be our cluster was decided, and the make of our shells designed. The particular setting for our personal story to hatch—the timing of it, the location, the people involved, the heritage, genetic code, the economy, the government and social strata were all seen and chosen in the deep.

Some of us may have just gained a new appreciation for the complex dynamic of an oyster reef, having grown up with "gnarly shapes" of our own breed. But before we blame oyster parents for the gnarly shaped children formed in their cluster, consider the conditions they grew up in themselves. Remember they have places that have been hidden in the deep for many years and have been gnarly shaped by the cluster that came before them as well. After years of being in the deep, oysters form a rough and tough exterior, usually from barnacles and other sea creatures. There are a host of influences that shape the minds of those who came before us—and though we may instinctively want to cast blame wondering what is wrong with them, it may be more effective to ask instead, what happened to them.

To be fair, we were not in their shoes when events took place in our world that rocked them, or in their worlds when events took place that wounded them. Though we may come from them, or were nurtured and raised by them, we were and are not actually them. Often, we are actually quite different from them, and judging what we don't understand gets us no closer to understanding them or ourselves any better.

It is wise, then, to move slowly and exercise a little empathy as we briefly look at our families of origin. We see circumstances much clearer in hindsight and are removed from the pressures of the moment when the parenting was done, or not done.

All this being said, we are not making excuses for their choices. Looking intently at the formation of our cluster is an undeniably profound step in the journey of understanding our story. Profound in the sense that we may discover things that were not true that we believed to be true at one point, because of what we learned from, or perceived about our clusters. We may have even based our major life's decisions on those perceived truths; after all, who would question their cluster? It is the entire framework for understanding the deep of God and ourselves.

In a sense, the Bible is the record of humanity through the line of one family. From Adam to Seth, to Abraham, and all the way through the people of Israel until the birth of Jesus, one lineage is recorded. I'm going to take a slight detour about this focus on family for a moment to say something about the recording of this lineage. After I did a timeline of the book of Genesis, I discovered that Noah was born approximately 120 years after Adam died. Lamech, Noah's father, had first hand testimony from the first man to ever walk on the earth with God in the cool of the day. Imagine then the power of these words Lamech spoke over his own son Noah:

> "This one will comfort us concerning our work and the toil of our hands, because of the ground which the Lord has cursed."

> —GENESIS 5:29

The curse was such a trauma. I wonder if Adam cried with Lamech over the loss of the Garden before he passed away. I wonder if this is what was on Lamech's mind when he saw his own first-born son enter this cursed earth, inspiring his vision for Noah.

Then there's Joseph and his older brothers, the brothers who later put Joseph in a well. Joseph's brothers were born while Shem still walked the earth, the same earth he floated high above in an Ark! One of Joseph's brothers, Levi, later became the great-grandfather of Moses. Though Moses didn't meet his great-grandfather personally, Moses was informed of the history of the earth by those who potentially spoke with Ark-riders, who spoke with those who spoke with the first human being on the planet. Why am I talking about this? Because what we have recorded in Scripture is trustworthy testimony. The long lives of our early patriarchs allowed for first-hand eyewitness accounts of the major events surrounding the beginning of our humanity.

Now back to family. Family was God's original creation for how humans relate to one another, so it is no surprise that God's enemy would seek to destroy the family at every turn. In the book of Exodus, the people of God were given a short list of commandments they were to live by in order to live well in relationship with God and each other. The curse had put a wall between the Creator and His creation, and a system of rules and sacrifices was the first phase of God's big redemption plan. Among those commandments was one that is often used to keep us from sharing the painful parts of our cluster:

"Honor your father and your mother, that your days may be long..."

—EXODUS 20:12

Even recently I heard of a pastor using this Scripture to keep his grandchildren from distancing themselves from his son, their father. The father had recently abandoned the family, admitted to deep addictions, unlawful behavior, infidelity, and was refusing to seek help, but the grandfather used this Scripture to suggest they were commanded by God to maintain a close relationship with him no matter his choices.

I too withheld introspection into my family of origin for years, afraid that I would somehow betray my family who worked hard to feed me and didn't physically abuse me like other women I know. But ignoring what is in our cluster does not protect our cluster from dishonor, nor does it help our story honor God. In fact, denial of how our cluster has shaped our shell, and how our shell has shaped us, can lead us on an unintended path marked more by shame than grace.

Dr. Sandra Wilson, in her book *Released from Shame*, presents essentially a treatise on how shame is passed down, even unintentionally in relatively healthy families, but also how to choose a better way. On the subject of whether to examine the impact of our families of origin, she explains:

> "In Exodus 20:12 God instructs us to 'honor' our fathers and mothers. In the original language, one aspect of the word for honor literally meant to be heavy. Eventually it meant to consider persons weighty, important or honorable, as in the case of city officials. With that word picture in view, it seems to me that we are honoring our parents when we consider their heavy influences in our lives. To ignore the weight of their examples and influences would be dishonoring our parents."[13]

Examining our families of origin does not mean we set out to blame our parents for all our problems, but that we are choosing to have truth establish our foundation for living. Truth is what we seek when we look back, so we can better make future decisions.

Each of us have hidden places with stories actively rolling in our minds that are not true, not helping us become who God intended us to become, and yet unless we bring them into the light of truth with God, we will never have the chance to exchange them for His truth. While we cannot change how our families of origin impacted us, or make others change, we can bring our stories to God to weigh out and seek His help in sorting lies from truth.

And I caution here, this is a *brief* look back. There is very little good that comes from living a past-focused life. If looking back at the stories of your origin causes heightened anxiety, deep negative emotions, or confusion, it is wise to consider doing this with a reputable professional Christian therapist or mentor. There is no shame in seeking truth, and this is what we are after! Jesus came to free us, to bind up our wounds, not our stories.

"And you shall know the truth, and the truth shall make you free."

—JOHN 8:32

MY REDEMPTION STORY

I learned a lot about what God does not say in Scripture, before I began to learn what He does say. By the age of ten, I probably visited a dozen different churches, ranging from snake-handlers to the liturgical sit-and-stand types. Some told us we'd have to change our hair and clothes, some told us to come as we are, and the messages about God continued to form through all my varied experiences within my shell. I watched my mom though, and went where she told me to go, even if I didn't want to or didn't understand what was being said. I loved the singing though, when we would sing hymns, or about Jesus and God, something in me wanted to know more, to sing more. I didn't want to play the games with other kids, I wanted to sit with adults and listen to what the speaker was saying, I wanted to know what church and faith and the Bible were about.

In 2005, I was privileged to be at my grandmother's bedside when she went Home to be with Jesus. My "Mommom" had only confirmed with me a year earlier, after we watched the movie *The Passion of the Christ* together, that she believed Jesus was God's Son and had died for her sins. I remember her hand rest on my shoulder in the car. She was sitting in the backseat. She patted me and told me, "Heather, I believe all that. I will see Jesus. I'm not afraid to die." Her death remains one of the most painful and powerful moments involving my family experience so far, and in part it was because of what I believed about my family, God and myself.

As I will share in the chapters coming, there were cuts inflicted in my soul early on in my life that left me feeling unsafe in this world. One of several sources of comfort and stability for me, including my mother and grandfather, was Mommom. She built into me a love for being a girl, for dressing feminine, standing strong and yet relating gently with others. She was lovely to me, and treated me like I was lovely, though I wouldn't think this about myself for years to come.

If we had a family tradition, it happened thanks to Mommom. If there was good news to share, Mommom would tear up, she would hug and want to celebrate. If you were sick, she'd scratch your back, make you soup, pile you up on the couch with a TV tray full of all the best things. If you just needed someone to listen with both ears and both eyes, she was the one. She was Christmas, Easter, birthdays and back-to-school shopping to me. So when she lay there in the Hospice room, and the nurses told us to tell her she could go, I couldn't do it. When it was my shift with her, and my mom, uncle and Poppop left the room, I'd tell her to stay, to not leave me, that I needed her still. When they'd return and reassure her she could go, I'd stay quiet and pretend like I wasn't secretly dying with her.

The nurse said after two days that it was odd, that she must not feel she can let go because she was hanging on as barely as one could. Guilt washed over me, I believed I was the reason her suffering was delayed. I went outside and took a walk with God. In my tears I confessed what I was doing. I admitted my fear of losing her, of losing myself, of losing my hope for family and goodness in this life. Releasing her felt like cutting off my own leg. I literally couldn't form the words to say good-bye to her. As I sat on a curb that Sunday, Grandparents Day, with the sound of Sunday night football blaring out one of the nearby windows, I sensed God tell me to go back in and read Scripture over her. I had never read Scripture with Mommom, ever. I didn't know what to expect, but I figured it couldn't be too terribly awkward. She wasn't speaking anymore so I wouldn't know it if she did feel uncomfortable. I went back into her room and during my next shift I read Psalm after Psalm to her, until I reached this verse:

"I would have lost heart, unless I had believed that I would see the goodness of the Lord in the land of the living."

—PSALM 27:13-14

In that moment faith rose up within me that gave me hope that I would see goodness, yet, in this land of the living even after Mommom was gone. I closed the Bible and began to tell her of all the good things God was going to do in my life. I spoke of getting married, even though there wasn't a man in sight. I spoke of children, of writing and speaking, of living a full life. I went on about all the ways I believed I'd see goodness here, and then goodness in Heaven. I told her she could go on if she was ready, that I'd be okay. Within 20 minutes I think she believed me. I held her hands as she slipped away from our presence, into the presence of her Savior.

Hours, days and weeks after Mommom's passing God affirmed what had happened in my heart. In my childhood I had concreted my life onto my mother's and her mother's, out of fear of being abandoned and exposed. It is natural, but God created the family as a shadow to point us to His love for us. The stability and comfort I received from Mommom, I had actually been receiving from God, through her. The love for feminine expression I shared with Mommom, it too was from God, expressed through her life. I realized the needs I had that were being met by my family of origin were actually met by God, through them. And He is faithful. He assured me He would continue to meet my needs even after they were no longer around. So too, He would meet the needs I have that they never could and never can meet.

Before we end here, I know family of origin can be a painful topic for some. Many do not have any information about their biological beginnings, whether from loss, abandonment, adoption, and so on. Being parents through adoption, we value all the information we have for our child as if it were our own family history. It is our family history. From day one, our daughter has been told age-appropriate parts of her story. Her beginnings will be as normal to her as her belly button if we live out our commitment to her well. There are parts that will be hard for us to share, and for her to receive someday, but parents do hard things for their kids every day. Grieving is a part of living and loving, and we will make space for all of it. Ultimately, though, our knowledge of our biology is not what moves us into our destiny with Christ. The sovereign hand of God who saw us in the womb has set us apart for a work He has planned just for each of us. He has given us all we need to know in order to fulfill our purposes in this life through the Word and His Holy Spirit, and the companionship of the body of Christ. Seeking Him in these ways is the healthiest choice we can make to embrace our roots and become who we are meant to be.

After all, one does not need to be adopted to feel estranged from her biological story. Many of us who are not adopted still feel disconnected from our families of origin for various reasons. Ancestral search-based businesses seem to be in high demand, proving that information continues to be a prized commodity. We seek answers to questions we have vague understandings of and place our fragile hope in an answer to them we deeply long to hear.

Am I loved? Do I matter? Does my life have purpose?

We can live with gaps in our story easier if we know the answers to these basic human questions. But if we are unsure of these, the gaps in our stories can become our obsession.

I've taken these questions to the people who make up my cluster, and in spite of their well-meaning efforts to answer them in an affirming way our clusters' answers are still inadequate.

There is a sign I keep up in my office to remind me that the people who made up my cluster are humans, with their own clusters.

"Just because someone doesn't love you the way that you want them to, doesn't mean they don't love you with all they have."

The hard thing about living with humans is that *all we have* just isn't enough for *all we need*. In Romans 3:23 we get some bad news that we have suspected all along, "…all have sinned, and fall short of the glory of God." We are all lacking, impaired, and unable to be perfect parents for our children. So even if my people knew how to do better, they just didn't have it in them to meet all of my needs.

From our very beginning, we have needed God to meet all our need. He is the Creator of the first cluster, the Master of the vineyard who alone can graft us into the vine, the oyster diver who alone can take us out of the deep sin sea and deliver us into safe waters.

But our clusters are not alone in the deep. There is another that lurks, a danger, and we know it in our soul.

DISCUSSION QUESTIONS
2—THE CLUSTER

YOUR REDEMPTION STORY

How would you describe your cluster? Who were the key players in your growing up experience? Where did you grow up? What generation were you in and how did that shape your view of your world, yourself and God?

_____

_____

_____

What messages did you learn about God from your cluster?

_____

_____

_____

What are some messages you've received about God from your family of origin that may not be in line with God's Word? This may take some time, be patient. Also, I highly recommend Dr. Sandra Wilson's book, "*Released from Shame—Moving Beyond the*

Pain of the Past," if you are having a hard time distinguishing truth from perception.

_____

_____

_____

We know that sometimes trauma occurs within the cluster, and there is pressure to keep silent about it. At any time, if unbearable pain surfaces for you emotionally, seek the care and counsel of a professional in your area. Contact a local church for a referral to give you a good place to start, but do not try to manage the pain on your own. God created the body with varying functions, so it can work together as a system to bring healing. The same is true for His Church. It is healthy to feel your pain, but there is a wise way to go about it and leaning on others to guide you through it can be enormously helpful. Be kind to your soul!

OTHER REDEMPTIVE STORIES

How has God used your family of origin to help you understand His nature as the perfectly good Father? How have you seen His love demonstrated through them? How have you seen His perfection filling their gaps?

_____

_____

_____

How has your family of origin responded to your faith journey with Christ? How has their response hindered or helped your faith to grow?

_____

_____

_____

the Irritant

"He was a murderer from the beginning,
and does not stand in the truth, because there is no truth
in him. Whenever he speaks a lie, he speaks from his own
nature; for he is a liar, and the father of lies."

—JOHN 8:44

There is a shadow in the water—I know it in my being. To have even survived to adolescence was a constant fight against fish and feeder. Many of my siblings never found a safe place to land. Yet even now, as I grow thicker in my middle and tougher along my edges, my design is giving me concerns. I have the ability to protect myself, but why? I can clamp and snap my shell shut by the way of these wondrous adductor muscles, and I have this fluid building up in me mysteriously. It is as if my form is built with guardians in place. I am not sure what the danger is, all I know is at some level I must be on guard.

There is talk of predators, different kinds in different places. The boring sponge, oyster drill and whelk that gradually bore through your shell into the flesh, either killing or consuming you, then often taking up residence in your shell. Crabs, lobsters and fish with their *brute strength of claw or teeth can crush and consume. Oyster toadfish, the stealthy bottom dwellers in camouflage that lay waiting for their prey. They are shady, living under rocks, in vegetation and wrecks during summer months, but hidden within oyster reefs all other times of year. Shaped like a leaf, oyster flatworms target primarily oyster spat (babies) and eat the meat of our young when we open our valves to feed. An oyster has to eat! Starfish are especially creative and penetrate our flesh and (prepare yourself) begin inserting their entire stomach inside of the oyster to begin digesting through chemical consumption. Can you imagine? And the salt, so I'm a bit high maintenance because I'm sensitive to salt levels, they have to be just right. Barnacles, starfish, mussel spat and other organisms will hamper our growth as well. So what cannot kill us will just keep us from thriving, I guess. I've heard exposing us to air (whatever that is) or washing us (something the grown-ups talk about), can kill off these destructive organisms.[14] Sounds amazing, but how can a simple oyster like me get there?*

But as anxious as these threats make me, the thing that has me awake at night is the story I hear about only in hushed tones. There's talk of an irritant in the waters, undetectable and subtle. Apparently, it can come in many forms, maybe a piece of betraying shell, coral, or even a parasite. Though not all irritants lead to death, they can still cut our flesh and create a wound. Apparently, one cut can be all it takes. While an oyster can survive and live with some wounds, over time the burden grows within our shells and can force us to pry open, exposing us to more danger and death. At least I can feel the whelk's drill or see the lobster's claw. At least I can clamp and snap against some of my foes. But how can I protect myself from such a sneaky enemy like the irritant?

I guess you could say I knew about evil before I really knew about God. Maybe it was this awareness of evil that gave me curious hope of there being a Hero.

As a young child, I felt safe if my mom was around. Mom made sure we ate, listened to us about school, asked who we were playing with and had rules about the television. She had rules about a lot of things, really. When mom wasn't around, rules weren't as much either. You would think this freedom would be freeing, but freedom is backwards sometimes. Good rules protect us from harm, and actually make it possible to experience true freedom. In a way then, maybe it was the rules that made me feel safe.

I watched my first scary movie before I could read. I didn't understand what was happening, but it terrified me. Something switched in my pre-K brain that day, and suddenly everything felt dangerous, from the neighbor to the pretty dolls in my bedroom. That's when I remember the nightmares starting, and fear of the dark, strangers, being alone, being kidnapped, of everything. There was a shadow, I knew it in my being, but I didn't understand what it, or who, it was.

I struggled with anxiety, and the reason I know is because of one night in particular.

I was about six years old, sleeping in my room when suddenly I woke up and couldn't breathe. I tried to scream for my mom but couldn't get it out. Something was pressing against my chest. I tried to see but it was all dark, I couldn't make anything out, but my chest was tight and felt crushed under a weight. Lights came on under the door, I could hear my parents coming toward my room. My parents opened the door, a light shone like a high beam against the darkness in my room, a white roadway at the end of my bed leading to safety. My mom must've noticed my trouble breathing because she immediately ran to collect her things. I could hear keys jingling, we were heading to the hospital. My dad sat in a chair at the end of my bed though, watching through the door at her scurrying around. He seemed tired and disoriented. I tried to sit up, to see him sitting there, but all I could see was a dark shadow like a boulder sitting on my stomach. I tried to look around it, I wondered if I was imagining it, but I remember thinking that something was sitting on me—I could almost make it out.

The next thing I knew I was having an EKG on my chest so they could check my heart for an arrhythmia. I felt like my chest had a balloon swelling up inside and was about to burst. My mom and I waited, and waited, as you do. Finally, the doctor came to discuss the results, but when he did he had my mom step aside, and pulled the curtain. I'll never forget the question, because I didn't understand what in the world it had to do with my chest pain.

"How are things in your home?" he asked.

My mom was furious. In fairness, she was terrified I was dying, and what you want is answers and good news, "Ok, it's this and it's easily fixable." You don't want a vague question when your child is struggling to breathe, and you definitely don't want to talk about how life hasn't turned out the way you dreamed.

"Ma'am, I understand you are upset, but what Heather is experiencing is anxiety."

That's how I know I struggled with anxiety as a child. And ever since, really.

I don't believe it was just the scary movies that fueled my anxiety. My life had some real life scary stories too.

I was four years old when I went on vacation with my grandparents. We were traveling from south Florida to Wisconsin to visit my great-grandparents. It was a long trip, especially back in the late 1970s with maps and back roads. We overnighted in Georgia in a hotel. The room had two full beds. I slept with Mommom while Poppop took the other bed. In the middle of the night I woke to a sound. When I opened my eyes, I saw two men in the front of the room hovering over the dresser, filling their pockets. One walked toward the closet, and the other made his way slowly toward me, walking up the aisle between the beds. I was sleeping toward the aisle, and could see him getting closer, when all of a sudden I must have closed my eyes and feigned sleep. Except, I actually did fall asleep. The next thing I remember is waking up to the lights on, news on the television, static beeps on walkie-talkies, and Mommom crying on the edge of our bed. I yawned and rubbed at my eyes and must have muttered out a question as to what was going on because Poppop then explained that we had been robbed. Then I remembered everything. I said, "Oh yeah, I know about that! I saw them! There were two men..." and I went on to describe what happened. I gave all the details I knew as they wrote everything down and looked at each other. I apparently affirmed what they had already been surmising. They later determined a former employee was behind it and had accessed a key. They didn't have to use a claw or a drill, they just slid right in undetected.

An irritant. How can you protect yourself from such a sneaky enemy like the irritant?

From then on when I prayed at night, "Now I lay me down to sleep, I pray the Lord my soul to keep. If I should die before I wake..." I wondered if that night was the night I'd die. The robbers in that hotel room injured me but not in a physical way. Their infliction worked its way into my soul a wound that would take me years to understand how to fend off...

Fear.

"But I am afraid that, as the serpent deceived Eve by his craftiness, your minds will be led astray from the simplicity and purity of devotion to Christ."

—2 CORINTHIANS 11:3

The senior pastor at my church likes to point out, "How do you know if you are being deceived? You don't."[15] That's the problem with deception. And that was the problem in the Garden. The ruin started with a lie, a half-truth. It always does.

But before we give Eve a hard time, remember the empathy we practiced as we looked back at our cluster? We need to show it to Eve too! Nothing like this had happened to her before. She was not expecting a serpent, or a voice, or an opposition to God. She didn't expect that someone with a key to the place would use it to come in and cause harm. From the text in Genesis 3, it appears Eve was cornered while she was alone. As perfect as she may have been, she was vulnerable to the charm and cunning of this irritant.

Eve was deceived by the irritant himself, once an angel of light by the name of Lucifer, now a bitter, exiled, proud and angry spiritual being with a vendetta. Many interpreters find Ezekiel's funeral lament for the king of Tyre as also containing a description of Lucifer, or Satan, himself. King Tyre's sin was that of pride and self-exaltation, and at the least was certainly driven by the influence of Satan.

"You were the seal of perfection,
Full of wisdom and perfect in beauty.

You were in Eden, the garden of God;
Every precious stone was your covering...

You were the anointed cherub who covers;
I established you;
You were on the holy mountain of God;
You walked back and forth in the midst of fiery stones.
You were perfect in your ways from the day you were created,
Till iniquity was found in you...

Your heart was lifted up because of your beauty;

You corrupted your wisdom for the sake of your splendor;
I cast you to the ground,
I laid you before kings,
That they might gaze at you.

You defiled your sanctuaries
By the multitude of your iniquities,
By the iniquity of your trading;
Therefore I brought fire from your midst;
It devoured you,
And I turned you to ashes upon the earth
In the sight of all who saw you.
All who knew you among the peoples are astonished at you;
You have become a horror,
And shall be no more forever."[16]

Satan was a former wonder, mighty in beauty, power and artistry. Moses, Isaiah, and Ezekiel give us insights into his character as cunning, proud, created with superior wisdom, a former resident in Eden, evil to the core, a liar, violent, and bent on being God. Paul, James and Peter give hope though, and explain that he has limits, and is not like God. He is not omniscient (all knowing), omnipresent (everywhere at once), or omnipotent (all powerful). But having some spiritual resources, he is certainly capable of creating sensually pleasing opportunities, including miracles to deceive unsuspecting people. His mission is to get God's created humankind to reject God, to twist His words, to oppose His work at every turn especially as it promotes the spread of His Gospel announcing eternal life is available to all who trust Christ for our sins!

His subtle twist of truth in his brief conversation with Eve wove several lies together to chisel away at her simple trust in God. But why should she doubt the One who was there when her eyes opened, welcoming her and bringing her into the company of a perfect man? The One whom her man trusted, who walked with them and provided in abundance? She had no reason, until this irritant, this serpent with a voice, suggested one.

Unraveling the deception, we find Satan suggesting that Eve had the authority of God to define what was good for her. Made in God's image, humankind was God's unique artwork with an ability to create. With an ability to reason and make decisions, Adam and Eve could rule the earth and think like designers and masters over creation, but with limits. The authority to define "good" remained with the Creator, and the Creator designated what was not good for humankind: isolation and consuming the knowledge of good and evil. Adam and Eve had creative liberties but did not have the authority to define what was essentially good in God's world.

Other lies were implied in Satan's deception too. His seed of doubt cast shadow over her confidence in knowing God's will. She's just easily confused and had it all wrong. Maybe she believed it's too difficult to understand what God wants and that she can't relate well with Him. And not God only, but she cannot relate well with her fellow human either. Satan's words may have worked mistrust of man's leadership into the woman's mind too. It could be that Eve didn't hear God's restriction of the tree directly from God, and only received the information from Adam. Now she couldn't trust herself to know God's will for her and she couldn't trust Adam to provide for and protect her either.

As the deceiver opened these channels of doubt in Eve's mind he released a venom: fear. For the first time the abundance she was surrounded with was not enough, at least that was what she was tempted to believe. The irritant's stealthy stab was to stoke a fear of missing out. This same lie implying God's boundaries deprive us of necessary good, has been driving humans to make destructive choices since the beginning of our history.

"Eve, if you don't eat this, you will miss out on being like God...and if you miss that, you miss..."

What was she missing, by the way? Nothing good. She was missing out on the knowledge of evil, which I could do without, thank you. God's limit, as it always is, was designed to protect Eve and Adam, to give them the fullness of joy and freedom and the bliss of heaven with Him. He was not, as Satan would have them believe, depriving them of some supremely good gift. God was setting them up for an eternal dream, but Satan was bent on eternal destruction, on smearing their human innocence with the smut of shame.

Present in the free will of humanity is the ability to not choose God. To not choose God is to choose for the self, and to thereby exalt self above God. It was this exaltation of self, this pride potential in Eve's free will and in all of us that got her in trouble. Just as God's truth has the activating agent within it to set free, lies have the activating agent to blind and bind.

"And you shall know the truth, and the truth shall make you free."

—JOHN 8:32

Jesus said of Satan in John 8:44, "...there is no truth in him. When he speaks a lie, he speaks from his own resources, for he is a liar and the father of it." By contrast God hates lies, He cannot lie, He loves truth. In fact, Jesus Himself *is* Truth.[17]

We see the sad effects of believing the father of lies play out tragically in the Garden. The first thing we notice is shame. All of a sudden what was completely good, acceptable, normal and a non-issue, is now seen through the lens of wrongness. Before Satan was believed nothing was wrong, nothing was broken. Now, something needed fixing, and if it couldn't be fixed, it needed to be covered, hidden and removed from sight. A fig leaf and twine could not restore what was lost in that scene. Shame would shadow their every step. The sad effects spiraled too. Shame wasn't the only wave to crash down on these new sinners.

Soon after shame pummeled, fear moved in and the true nature of Lucifer was revealed in fuller horror.

Now I'm going to step back for a bit, I hope you don't mind me going a little further into the theological woods. There are differing interpretations of the Scripture surrounding God's creation of the earth, and of His enemy's entrance into it. While the ultimate point I make in this chapter and in the entire book is unchanged by these differing views, I want to address them briefly but more importantly draw your attention to two themes. The first theme is loss. All of God's creation experienced a terrible loss of innocence and freedom through Satan's influence. As devastating as this loss is, contrasted with this loss is a second theme: God's redemption. Immediately we see God respond to the loss with passion and a plan. Loss doesn't win the headline. The book of Genesis gives us not only the first chapter of humanity but the last chapter as well. The hope displayed in the first human story will sustain us through this book and I think can carry us through the remainder of our lives!

Now to address just a couple of differing views of the creation account—one view is that the earth created in Genesis 1:1 continued to unfold uninterrupted for seven days and then remained unharmed (except for the curse) until the disastrous Flood. Satan preceded human life and had limited reign of the earth. Adam and Eve were placed together in the Garden where they were given authority to rule. Satan deceived God's first people, they disobeyed God bringing curse on the earth and only God could redeem what was lost.

Another view though is that the Earth created in Genesis 1:1 is not the same earth later created in Genesis 1:3. This "gap theory" for creationism relies on the differing words used to describe God's creating work. The word for "created" in verse 1 is "bara" meaning to "make out of nothing". Truly there was nothing, and then there was something—the heavens and the earth! In verse 2 though gap-theorists suggest something has happened to that earth:

> "...the earth was without form, and void; and darkness was on the face of the deep. And the Spirit of God was hovering over the face of the waters."

A "void" or "formlessness" is described by Isaiah and Ezekiel later as a divine destruction, possibly of a wrecked earth and of Lucifer's judgment in Isaiah 14:12, 17:

> "How you are fallen from heaven, O Lucifer, son of the morning! ... Who made the world as a wilderness and destroyed its cities..."

Gap-theorists say it was somewhere between these two earths, between Genesis 1:1 and 1:2, that Satan came to be and was prominent in beauty and power. Soon after though his mind was corrupted by it and he sought to be God, resulting in his ejection from the heavens to the earth, along with a selection of angels who followed his lead. At some point the fallen Lucifer brought on the destruction of the first created earth with his wickedness, and God set out on His plan to redeem the whole mess. This redemption of the earth would include a second creation account described in more detail starting in Genesis 1:2. This time the word used is not referring to God creating out of nothing ("bara") like in Genesis 1:1, because there is already material there from before. It was just ruined. Instead now God "forms" and "builds" and calls the earth to "give forth"[18] of the seed still present from the first beginning.

Regardless of how Satan came to be on the earth we inhabit today, two points remain the same: a grave loss was incurred in the Garden and God redeemed that loss through a grave.

Even if God did re-create the earth after Satan wrecked it once, God was not surprised by His need to do so. How can

God be surprised when He is all-knowing? He cannot. What we do know is that before the foundation of the earth there was a meeting of the minds, the high minds of God the Father, Jesus the Son and the Holy Spirit together, three in One. In 1 Peter 1:18-21, (with my emphasis added), we see how the sacrifice of God's only Son was always God's "Plan A" for Israel's redemption and for our salvation:

> "...you were not redeemed with corruptible things, like silver and gold, or from your aimless conduct received by tradition from your fathers (religious performance—"doing good"), but with the precious blood of Christ, as of a lamb without blemish and without spot. He indeed was foreordained before the foundation of the world, but was manifest in these last times for you, who through Him believe in God, who raised Him from the dead and gave Him glory, so that your faith and hope are in God."

Humankind was part of God's "Plan A". He desired a unique creature mixed of divine breath and dust of the earth. Satan would remain relentless, aiming always to wreck God's design but nothing thwarts God's purposes. People would bear seed of their own kind. Fathers would pass down traditions. And at the right time Christ would be born into the stream of humanity but would live without sin. He would die but then He would raise again from the dead. This was always God's original redemption plan, even before the beginning.

Satan cannot thwart God's ultimate plan and has limited reign; he cannot attack without permission, as we see in Job's account. God retains sovereignty and the fullness of His nature even as He delegates power to His creatures. But Lucifer is incredibly powerful, and his ultimate weapon is still doubt in God's Word. As we learn from the Garden, a seed of doubt is all it takes. God reminds us today in the book of Hebrews that it is our belief that matters:

"...without faith it is impossible to please God..."

—HEBREWS 11:6

Our belief is where Lucifer will take straight aim. He is the master counterfeiter, parading himself as a god, an answer for our emptiness, a false hope for those who feel the weight of shame. We believe that if we try harder, aim higher, do more, become perfect, do good enough, get more, beat ourselves down that we will raise ourselves up. He uses God's creation, His symbols, His principles, His people, His elements and even God's words twisted to deceive us.

Eve was cut by Lucifer's deception. Without understanding the full impact of her choice, she believed the father of lies and acted accordingly. She disobeyed God's command because that is what we do when we are deceived. While the irritant brought deception that would rub all of humanity, God foresaw the irritant's presence in the Garden, his trick of Eve, and the fall of His creation. In His mercy He hatched a plan and wrote out the final chapter for humanity. The prophesied Messiah, the Seed of Eve, would one day crush the serpent's head. God would take the irritation, the sin of the world, and would end it once and for all. Until then though, the snake would bruise His heel. His tactics: to cut and wound, to lie, steal and destroy. If the irritant could ensure it, this would be his mission:

"Behold, therefore, I will bring strangers against you,
The most terrible of the nations;
And they shall draw their swords against the beauty of your wisdom,
And defile your splendor.
They shall throw you down into the Pit,
And you shall die the death of the slain
In the midst of the seas.'[19]

The irritant tried to inflict on Eve and on each of us the very punishment that will rightfully come to him in time. This passage is actually God's future promise for Satan's own destiny. The lie of Lucifer brought shame, fear and anxiety. The truth in Christ brings grace, love and peace. The mastermind plan of God the Father, Jesus the Son and the Holy Spirit was and is in place, and the irritant knows it. While he lurks yet in the deep around us, his power and time is finite, and we have hope of overcoming his trickery in our lives:

> *"And they overcame him by the blood of the Lamb and by the word of their testimony..."*
>
> —REVELATION 12:11

Did you catch that? The blood of the Lamb is the sacrificial death of Jesus, whose blood has been shed for us. That part is finished; we'll talk more about that later. But did you see our part? We are to use our testimonies, share our redemptive stories that hinge on the Gospel of Jesus Christ. We may not always see it in the physical realm of our day-to-day life, but God's Word gives us assurance of victory over His enemy as we trust in the Gospel and its power. So friends, let us not live in fear of the one who hates us. May we share our redemptive stories centered on the Gospel and pass them down to those around us.

MY REDEMPTION STORY

As afraid as I was of the evil that I knew lurked in the dark, and even in my home at times, it wasn't fear that drove me to know God. Fear drove me, just to other places. The fear of rejection drove me as a child to be the funny kid in school, to make fun of myself and be the class clown so I could garner the approval of cool kids—or any of the kids—before they could reject me. Fear of failure drove me to do everything every teacher said, read every word, over-achieve on my homework and excel on projects. Fear of emotional pain, since I am a deep feeler, drove me to stuff my body with food it didn't need so I wouldn't feel the confusing grief over the loss of my innocence and the anxiety that was my nagging companion. Fear definitely drove me, but not to God.

I knew a devil existed, I knew his voice. I knew, in some way I didn't understand, I had him in me. I could be kind to others, but in the quiet place I knew I had something wrong in me that I was desperate to get out of me. I wasn't sure if being good would be good enough, so I tried to be great. At everything. Some days it felt like I was on the right track too, I felt pretty good about myself when I had great being-great days. The problem with this, though, was two-fold. One, they were great being-great days, but not perfect days. I'd always slip up somewhere, even if slightly, and I'd remember the deep haunt of wrongness in me. The other problem with this path was the exhaustion. I didn't recognize it as exhaustion, not as a kid, but it was there in my bitten-down nails, my anxiety, my secret binging, my chronic negative self-talk and the fearful way I covered my chest and stomach with my hands when I slept. See, I reasoned that if someone were to stab me in the middle of the night, the knife would have to go through my hand first and would have less impact on my vital organs. What kid thinks this way?

A frightened one.

Protecting myself from external irritants was an exhausting daily reality for me. But the worst of it was that I knew I had already been compromised on the inside, the wrong was with me, in me, and I could do nothing about it.

It is a common misunderstanding that when you put your trust in Jesus to forgive you of all your sin, you will no longer be vulnerable to the deceptive wiles of the devil. Alas, it can be quite the opposite. When we are adopted into the family of God and become entirely new people, born of a new nature, name and identity, we inherit all the treasures of Heaven and the same blessings of Christ Himself. We also, though, inherit His enemy. We are no longer children of Satan in our unbelief, we have been rescued from his prison walls, set free into marvelous light, and he hates it. No longer able to influence our forever home, he aims straight for our joy here and reward there. He uses his best tools, dangles the shiniest trinkets, hones the sharpest arrows, and strategically launches a battle plan against our soul. He has been watching us, observing our ways, our weaknesses, our fears, and knows what has worked in the past. We are safe in the Gospel of Jesus that will carry us all the way home to Heaven. This boat buoys above the waters of trial and stumbling like Noah's ark carried him above the waters of judgment, but we will still feel the swells and on somedays it will smell like stink all around.

"In this life, you will have trials..."

—JOHN 16:33

The irritant never leaves us alone, even if we have a redemption story of Christ saving us from sin. He continues to hound us, and even seems to double down efforts to prevent us from experiencing the joy of Christ's redemption in our lives. And he definitely works against us so we do not pass these stories down to others. For most of us though he doesn't come at us in obvious ways, with apples and floods. It is sly, discrete, a betraying half-truth about who we are and who God is, and before we know it we are in a choke-hold with shame.

The Word of God tells me I have the mind of Christ, which is stable, productive, sound, clear, creative, filled with truth and goodness and belief in God. The mind I experience has not always felt this way. It has been more like what the fields here in northeast Tennessee must have been like during the civil war, all turmoil and casualties. Scripture says in 1 Corinthians 2:16 that we have the mind of Christ at the moment we put our faith in Him. I assumed that if I had it I should automatically have new wonderful thoughts and attitudes! Since I didn't have wonderful thoughts and attitudes naturally, and still had terrible thoughts and attitudes, I concluded that I must not have the mind of Christ—or be saved. I'll share more about this later, but it took me years before I learned that enjoying the new mind Christ promises isn't automatic. While we instantly possess it at salvation, it is a mindset we must access and develop intentionally, like a muscle. There is no neutral thought, no thought sits still but moves us toward trusting God or trusting something else, always. The irritant knows this so at our mind he aims his best shots.

For the ones who live much of their day in their mind thinking constantly, like me, life is especially hard. Henri Nouwen says, "Our ability to think is our greatest gift, but it also the source of our greatest pain." Amen! Thinking new is a life-long neverending practice of redirection. It's like choosing to remove an old worn favorite pair of shoes and slipping on a new pair with arch support. The old shoes are what we know, we have a history and it's hard to let them go. We can own the new pair and never wear them, wondering all our lives why our feet and back are hurting. The best scenario is that we simply choose to take them off and put on the new. Oh, if I only applied this wisdom more quickly! For me though it involves reaching a pain point when I become desperate for a new way and then finally surrender to what God says in His Word on that matter. Believing God's ways are best gets easier as we experience His faithfulness, and this takes time like working in that new pair of shoes. It can feel weird and unfamiliar for a while but in time we find the stride is so much better in God's grace. You will adjust, new memories will be made and after a while you may even find that the old pair just doesn't fit you anymore.

I tried living in old shoes all the way through college. My mind was held hostage to wild emotions triggered by extreme circumstances and the irritant loved every minute. I'd read Scripture, but when I went to live life I'd react based on how I felt, which was not very good. I began to spiral especially in my sophomore year at the University of Notre Dame. I was desperate for an anchor, for truth. I wanted a way of living that was full of peace and God's power and not constant drama. God began a work in me that semester and rescued me from my downward spiral by drawing me into a deeper understanding of how the irritant works in my mind, and how I can take an active role in the battle.

One of the greatest influences for me in this "battle" being waged in my mind was Joyce Meyer. Her well-known book called *Battlefield of the Mind* helped me better understand what it means to put on the mind of Christ and walk in truth.[20] Joyce didn't originate the concept of the mind being a battlefield, there is nothing new under the sun. The apostle Paul wrote to the Christians in Rome about this battle:

> "...but I see in my members another law waging war against the law of my mind and making me captive to the law of sin that dwells in my members."

> —ROMANS 7:23

But Joyce's relatable writing helped me wake up in college to the importance of my chosen thoughts, and that I had the ability to choose them at all! I began practicing a new way of thinking, using God's Word as my guide. I found hope for a new life as I regularly slipped into my new mind with Christ—a mind filled with Scripture.

I also read C.S. Lewis's book *The Screwtape Letters* which illuminates the hidden efforts of Satan's minions to deceive, distract, discourage, detour and destroy what they can of God's beloved ones.[21] We are not uniquely broken just because we battle in our minds. There are present with us entities actively seeking to derail us.

A few years ago I made a decision that has helped me clarify the influence of these entities that work against my mind. I named the irritating voice in mind, the master deceiver that often shouts shameful thoughts into my everyday life. Since I'm a woman, it just fit to call the voice a her but gender is hardly the point here. The name I chose was *Scribble*, since often her influence creates emotional static, confusion, and stirs up a whirlwind of anxiety and fret making my next steps hard to discern. I wake with *Scribble*. Before I even get out of bed I have a page full of scribble marks in my mind spelling out shameful thoughts and stirring up stress. In order to clear the page and write new thoughts, I make time to be still with God's Word until His thoughts are all I see. But *Scribble* comes back throughout the day, so a practice for me has been to get still whenever I get overwhelmed, which has happened more times than I can count in this book-writing process! In that stillness I listen and identify what is from *Scribble*, and what is from God. Knowing God's Word is critical for this battle because often *Scribble* twists God's Word to get me even more confused! *Scribble* will seek to puff me up to be more than what God says, and then will level me to be less than what God says, sometimes all in the same lie. God will affirm who I am, and who He is, and will always steady my soul. Truth sets us free, every time.

I won't battle against *Scribble* forever, thanks to Jesus. I don't even battle *Scribble* constantly in the same areas as I have in the past. To the extent I have grown in knowledge of God's Word I have learned better how to fight in the battle for my mind. But agility is not immunity. A carefully slung slingshot to my identity could still take me down on an unsuspecting day, and so I learn to stay alert.

But ultimately, the devil is not my responsibility. My surrender to the mind of Christ is my daily responsibility, but that only. My belief in God, my belief in His truth, my belief in the finished work of Christ—this is my part. Our part. God has the irritant on His calendar.

> *"And the great dragon was thrown down, the serpent of old who is called the devil and Satan, who deceives the whole world."*
>
> —REVELATION 12:9

DISCUSSION QUESTIONS
3—THE IRRITANT

YOUR REDEMPTION STORY

Were you afraid of certain things growing up?

_____

_____

_____

What did you think of when you, *if* you, thought about evil, the devil, or Hell? Were you taught about them from a Biblical perspective?

_____

_____

_____

Do you understand who Satan is and what his role is in God's Kingdom plan?

_____

_____

_____

OTHER REDEMPTIVE STORIES

How has your fear drawn you closer to or hindered your growth with God?

_____

_____

_____

Share a time when you were stuck in lies in an area, struggling against shame, fear and anxiety; but God helped you find hope for grace, love and peace with His truth.

_____

_____

_____

the Cut

"There are circumstances where you cannot do anything.
It was only the Lord who has carried me through, and it's good
that I have experienced that. For I have always believed, now
I know from experience, that Jesus' light is stronger than the
deepest darkness. And a child of God cannot go so deep; always
deeper are the Everlasting Arms that carry you."

—CORRIE TEN BOOM

I have to breathe, there really is no way around it. If it weren't for these gills, I'd be a tomb. These gills are my bridge to the deep surrounding me, and they do the hard work of constantly filtering out a lot of what could, well, kill me. And it's the little things that can get in that can do some of the worst damage. My only way to guarantee no parasites, no tiny intruders, would be to not breathe. And that is no life at all.

You may think because I have no central nervous system like plants I've heard about, that I feel no pain. I'm not exactly sure what pain is, but I react when I'm hurt. You could say I groan here in my little shell. Does this count? If I am not feeling pain, it means I don't feel pleasure either, so I'm not sure I'm really winning on that account anyway.

It was just a matter of time before a cut would come my way. Not that I knew what it meant to be cut, but now that I look back it had happened to everyone in my cluster, all my friends and neighbors, at some point in some way. But that first cut shocked me, I wasn't prepared for it, I didn't understand what was happening. I was just minding my own business, was even surrounded in my cluster. I knew scary things lurked in the deep but up to that point life felt pretty easy. Then one day an irritant snuck in and suddenly alarms sounded within me. All the fluids began to course through me, rushing to my cut flesh, and I knew. Nothing would ever be the same.

In spite of my family joking that I had gills, I didn't really. I checked. But I did love swimming, and so does my daughter. The waters I swam in were clean, salty and see-through. I refused to swim in the dark bayous that worked in and out of our shoreline. I knew it wasn't dirt that made them dark, but just in case, I wanted to keep my gills clean and my body intact, and in the dark I couldn't see what swam nearby.

Though I didn't filter water through my little body growing up, I did filter experiences through my mind. Things happened, there were dark waters surrounding me as a child, and it was inevitable that something would work its way into me that didn't belong, that I would get cut just because I was swimming in them.

The first cut I can remember was when I was barely 4 years old, I was but a spat. We lived in Naples, Florida, and as was our routine I went with my dad to the local pier while he fished. It gave my mom time to work or clean or be sick as she was carrying my baby brother. I only remember a few instances of fishing with my dad in Naples. He told me about a time he was fishing with me along a shore and he hooked an alligator that came running toward us. It's good for both of us he was a fast runner. He snatched me up and took off. He also remembered a time when we went to put the car through a car wash, but when he went to get me out of the car realized the door was locked. He panicked, naturally, begging me through the window to push the button to lower the window. I just laughed at his silly faces, clueless. On all such occasions, I obviously survived, but there was one story that didn't turn out so well, one that neither he nor my mom would know about for many years.

One of my dad's fishing friends joined in on our fishing days together quite often. I don't remember him much, but my dad liked him. On one occasion, we went to his house for a visit, which must not have been for long because I don't remember eating and I certainly would have eaten if too much time passed. I did use the bathroom though because I can remember my legs dangling over the edge of the standard adult-size toilet. Across from the toilet was a brown wicker hamper, probably for holding toilet paper or towels, but on the top was a stack of magazines. My mom loved magazines. We had them scattered around at our house reminding us of the season we were in, of the foods we'd love to eat, recipes we had to try, crafts that seemed easy but never were, stately homes with fine furnishings and the buzz on fashion. I loved the artful layouts and read every word cover to cover, often sitting next to my mom if I could. It only took moments though for me to realize that these weren't like my mom's magazines. Far from it. It was as if the images on the pages gave off a toxic gas that caused the blood to rush to my dizzying head. My stomach twisted and tangled up and began to cramp as the room seemed to fill with a dark and thick vapor, like choking diesel exhaust from my dad's cherry red Chevy Vega. I rushed out and we left. We even moved to another city. I never saw my dad's fishing buddy again or went back to his house. I also never spoke to anyone about those magazines, though they continued to speak dark things to me. And at unexpected times.

The phone rang. I was only around 7 years old now and was home alone with a visiting aunt on my dad's side of the family. I answered it and gave the man on the other end my name because he asked for it. The next words I heard didn't make sense, but the sound in his voice registered familiar in my soul. It was the dark and dirty voice I heard in the magazines. My aunt must've seen the blood drain from my face because before I knew it she had cleared the living room, snatched the phone out of my hand and began a hostile rant of forceful words I didn't recognize into the receiver. They were all in Spanish. She asked me what he said when she hung up and I started to shake. I told her, but the words themselves seemed harmless except when strung together and said to a female child—they were all wrong. Her brows furrowed deep, and eyebrows arched high like pointed rooftops, something I share with her and my dad's face. She went back to whatever she was doing but I went to my bedroom, crawled under the covers and feared the voice. Now he knew my name. I thought he would come to the house any minute now and take me. I took a little toy baton and put it under my bed just in case I needed a weapon.

A couple years later, around age 9, we were over at my grandparents' house. They were retired military and built a small house immediately outside an air force base. I loved that house. I had the best memories growing up in that house, and of my grandparents. They were a haven for me and provided me with a sense of safety and stability that I needed desperately. One afternoon though my grandparents' house became my safe house in a whole new way.

My brother and I were playing ball in the backyard, having a great time. The yard felt like a football field to us, but was only probably 500 square feet, at the most. That's the way of it for kids; things can seem so different than they are in reality. I forget whether it was my brother or I who launched the ball clear over the back fence, into the back-neighbor's yard. We didn't know them, we only knew the neighbors to the right side of the house. There were no neighbors on the left side of my grandparents' house because they owned a corner lot. A major road edged their property carrying wealthy people the next block ahead into a separated community with a much higher average home value. The community had the word "Lake" in it and entering it felt like entering a magical world. I would daydream of living there, or in a community with a name.

As the big sister I took the role of retriever of all missing balls, so I went out the metal lattice gate, skipped through the grass along the busy road, and walked up to the front door of the back-neighbor's house. A teenage boy opened the door. He had glasses on. I explained why I needed to get in his back yard, and he obligingly let me in. Without any conversation I quickly went straight back to the glass sliding doors, which were like the ones in my grandparents' house. The ball sat in plain sight, so I hurled it back over the fence to my brother. I turned onto the concrete slab patio and stepped up through the glass doors when I looked up to thank the boy. It took a moment for my eyes to adjust from sunshine to darkness, but soon I noticed the boy standing with nothing on but his glasses. It seemed odd to me, and for a split-second I tried to remember if he had clothes on when I walked in before. I started to reason why he would need to take his clothes completely off when he charged at me. I knew his reasons were anything but good, so I ran. All of a sudden the house turned into a labyrinth of winds and turns and dead-ends. I kept wondering where the blasted door was—it had seemed like a simple house layout and straight shot from the back glass sliding doors. I ended up cornered in a peach bathroom. I hate peach. If he said anything to me, I don't remember it. In my deepest instinct all I knew to do was kick as hard as I could. I grabbed the doorknob with my right hand and propped up on the sink counter with my left hand and high step kicked with my eyes closed like a wild animal. I must've made contact too, because I was soon through that door and then out of the front door sprinting scared the short run to my grandparents' house outpacing the cars whizzing by to paradise. I feared he was going to chase and catch me, but I made it into the house and then collapsed on the living room floor heaving tears onto the camel brown carpet. My heart was racing, as was my mind. I was fearful of physical harm, but was also confused and disgusted, and embarrassed. Deeply embarrassed. As my mom and grandmother begged me to tell them what was wrong, I felt nauseous at the thought of telling them the truth, of saying the word naked and boy together. I did finally get enough words out for them to call the police, and apparently by the time they arrived no one was home. The house was vacated the very next day.

Around this same time my family lived in a house across the street from a neighbor who had a granddaughter, also named Heather. She was "little Heather" and I was "big Heather". The names helped distinguish us I'm sure, but there is much that went into my little soul with those descriptions. Little Heather's mother wasn't around much, she took different jobs like different boyfriends and was in and out of Little Heather's life. Her grandparents were more like her parents, unless her mom was staying for a while, usually with a new guy. I never saw her mom's boyfriends, but I knew they left things behind like movies, and memories for Little Heather that must have been confusing. She was a nice girl, she would share with me and laugh and seemed to enjoy my company. She also had odd curiosities, or so I thought. She would like to role-play scenes from movies, and her scenarios tended to be uncomfortable and ended up with touching that seemed wrong. I didn't understand why it was wrong, why we were playing this way, why we shouldn't be playing this way. I just knew I felt dark and dirty. The thick diesel exhaust seemed to fill the room again, choking me until I just had to go home.

By the age of 10, I had been exposed to cuts in many ways: dangerous men, dangerous spaces, dangerous neighbors and dangerous friends. There were other instances, not as dramatic, but still damaging nicks were set into my soul. All the while, I remember beautiful stories too: fun trips with my grandparents and parents to Disney World; breakfast time with my mom dancing while she prepared delicious hot food; the comforting rhythm of spending the night with my grandparents on Friday nights with our special routines; and, many joyful nights playing Frisbee or hide-and-seek with other wonderful neighbor kids. Growing up I generally felt like a loved kid, like someone who mattered. It wasn't all sad and scary. And because of the good times I would ignore the cuts, deny they existed as best as I could. To acknowledge them felt like betraying the ones trying to love me. Sharing how I had been cut could make them feel terrible about not protecting me. I didn't want them to feel terrible. Not like I felt.

I didn't know then just how those cuts had worked their way into my heart, and what would come from them. Another woman lacked this same vision when she too was cut by a lurking evil irritant.

"God, your God, will cut away the thick calluses on your heart and your children's hearts, freeing you to love God, your God, with your whole heart and soul and live, really live."

—DEUTERONOMY 30:6

Looking again at our epic beginning in the Garden of Eden, we see the cut clearly displayed, although not so clear to our foremother, Eve. Again, it's easy in hindsight to see how those who came before us erred. We don't look back to judge, but to learn from, so let's look at the cut, and how it works in us today.

The irritant entered the shell of Eden with a deceiving twist to tangle the mind of Eve and Adam, creating just enough mistrust in God to take action. It is this twist, this lie spoken with words out of a serpent's mouth, an act of treason, this call to coup, a violent trauma against the perfect inerrant word of God, that worked its way into Eve's shell and cut her belief in God. This deception, a seed of doubt, was the first cut on the earth. Though all the irritant can really do is cut us with deceit, that's all it takes to get trouble started. Shame, fear, blame and the negative effects of the curse on our earth soon follow.

There is a difference, though, between an oyster and Eve. Well, there are many differences really. Where Wild Pearl, our oyster friend, has flesh intact uncut from her beginning, we are daughters of Adam and Eve. As descendants of their kind, we are born already bearing the federal head's cut in us: sin.

Adam and Eve were created perfectly, with perfect minds of exceeding intelligence. From their progeny would come the minds of Michelangelo, Mozart, Einstein and every recipient of the Nobel Prize. Unimaginably better though, Adam and Eve had nothing to corrupt their minds and were made to live forever. They could invent, create, design, imagine, build, and organize with perfect precision and endless creativity. Imagine what Einstein could have devised by the age of 900 had he been undistracted by any temptation on this earth?

Moreover, Adam and Eve were given reign over the whole earth and were at home in a perfect Garden with ideal weather conditions, no inflammation of joints, no aging, no stress, strain or shame. Instructed to replenish the earth, to fill it again with their kind, humanity was intended to flourish in perfection forever. The nature of their children would be as they were, perfect before God the Creator. But their nature changed with the act of rebellion, the DNA became corrupted and aging began immediately. The "kind" they once were would never be again in this life. From that point on, their offspring would bear the new nature, with the knowledge of good and evil, with sin conscience that separated them from a Holy God. This is the "kind" we still are at our human birth, we are the new strand of humanity, post-apple. So we, unlike Eve or the first oyster, were born already cut, our very nature already compromised, in need of a do-over. We are born in need of a Savior.

God is working out His redemptive story for humankind. Cuts will be for a time here in the land of the living, but justice will come. In a sense, it has already begun.

"For evildoers shall be cut off; But those who wait on the LORD, they shall inherit the earth."[22]

We will not experience the cut of trials and suffering in this life forever. Our time is limited and the ones who are causing the pain will be held accountable. We can take great comfort in knowing that God is fully aware and awake to our pain, at work healing and restoring us constantly. It is God's faithfulness that helps us not live in fear of cuts. In fact, God even allows some of the cuts in our stories as His way of pruning off of us what steals life from us.

"For the word of God is living and powerful, and sharper than any two-edged sword, piercing even to the division of soul and spirit, and of joints and marrow, and is a discerner of the thoughts and intents of the heart."[23]

God can use the pain of trials in our lives to heal our souls from the barnacles and whelks that are working their way into our lives. He knows our thoughts, our motives, our desires and fears. Remember the problem with deception is we don't know if we are deceived. But God knows the compromises we are apt to make, the distractions we entertain that take us away from who we are called to become. God knows the relationships that hinder our growth and cause us to stray. Sometimes the grace of God comes to us in a cut to protect us. The grace is a pain allowed that triggers alarms and helps us receive the rushing aid of God's

Spirit, renewing our minds in truth and restoring our focus to what is eternal. No matter how the cut comes though, whether well-intentioned or not, God immediately sets about working it into a grander work we may only understand in part during our lifetime.

MY REDEMPTION STORY

As I shared earlier, I knew that there was wrong in me, in some form. I couldn't put my finger on where the cut came from, what it was exactly, but I knew I had dirt in me I couldn't wipe clean. The cuts that came in my early years only reinforced this sense of wrongness. As I internalized other's sins against me as my own sin, (yet without knowing what sin even was), I grew more hopeless in ever being freed from the haunting sense of doom and weight of disgust I carried in my young soul. I felt powerless to be pure and lovely, I also felt powerless to protect myself against more cuts. All this "powerlessness" added up to me being one angry young girl who felt dirty. If I didn't inflict my anger on the bullies on the P.E. field, especially against boys named "Brandon", I'd inflict it against myself in self-rejecting attitudes, bitten-down nails, eating binges, and then would whip myself into more attempts to achieve perfection in my performance as a daughter, student and friend. On the surface I looked like a good girl, a smart girl, a funny girl, a happy girl, but on the inside a battle was raging, and I wasn't sure how I was going to ever have peace.

I mentioned my sophomore year in college when I talked about the irritant. It was a bittersweet season between God and I—I was bitter in rebellion, and it took a deep cut to get my attention and return my heart to my first love. I was nineteen, and in a relationship headed for marriage. The problem was that I was a wreck in my soul, and the guy I was in a relationship with had his own wreck but neither of us were dealing with our stuff.

In short, we were drama.

I was a pre-professional science major, and music minor under constant pressure to perform at a high standard, whether that was in a marching band, in character, or in academics. I was trying hard to be good, do good, make good grades, but I was cracking under that pressure and was putting all my worth and hope in the relationship with the boyfriend. I had wounds I didn't understand yet and was reacting to my pain emotionally. Though I belonged to Christ and had the Holy Spirit within me, I had made so many choices over time that gave power to the boyfriend or others to tell me who I was and whether I was worthy of love, it was hard to reorient back to what God said about me in His Word.

So God cut me by cutting the boyfriend out of my life.

"Every branch in Me that does not bear fruit He takes away; and every branch that bears fruit He prunes, that it may bear more fruit."

—JOHN 15:2

The details aren't important, but our relationship ended. He moved on and I was heartbroken. I spiraled for a while in hopelessness and pain, but it was more of a detox of my soul than a true perishing. After releasing some toxic emotions through fitful and honest sobbing prayers in my dorm room (missing some chemistry labs), God began to mend the place of the cut. The raw tender place began to heal slightly, I started to listen to what God was saying in His Word again, and He even gave me an insight into what had transpired. In the gentlest way God showed me the image of a garden, filled with thorns and thistles, weeds and bramble bushes tangled and decaying. Nothing about the scene was lovely, and it looked like I had felt for a long time. Somehow I knew He was telling me that giving authority to any person to give me worth was like sowing weed seed in the garden of my soul. What I sowed, I reaped, and it was worthless. He gave me rich hope that He wanted me to partner with Him in a new kind of planting. With His help I could take the seed of His Word about me into my mind, I could water it with praise and life-giving meditation, I could surround the seed with the fresh air of community with other Christians seeking growth, and He restored my hope that I could have a thriving soul.

I wasn't sure Jesus could really help me change, to be honest. But the alternative definitely had not worked. As I tested the Lord by simply doing what He told me to do—filling my mind with His Word, reading it, studying it, singing it, thinking about it, writing about it, and joining community with other Christians, I noticed a change in me I had longed for but didn't know how to make happen. I wasn't the only one who noticed either. Not only did my friends start seeing the change, so did the boyfriend who came back into my life seeking a second chance. Though I gave it to him, and things were different enough that we even got engaged, God cut him out of my life again before marriage. Just in the nick of time God revealed to me again how this was not His best plan for us and we were about to make a mistake. As hard as it was to end that relationship, again, I look back and see His goodness in it all—for both of us.

God wanted more for me than I could have ever planned for myself. That's God's way too. If He cuts something from us, it is only to make space for something else He wants for us that is richer, deeper, better than we could have planned for ourselves. The irritant cuts us to bind us. God uses the cuts to free us—more and more.

DISCUSSION QUESTIONS
4—THE CUT

YOUR REDEMPTION STORY

Did you feel like something was wrong with you growing up?

_____

_____

_____

When did you first learn you were born with a cut already working in you? (A sin nature…)

_____

_____

_____

OTHER REDEMPTIVE STORIES

If you have breath, you have felt the cuts of sin in this life. Share some that have been instrumental in driving you toward God and His Word.

_____

_____

_____

How have the cuts of sin, yours or others' in your life, helped shape who you are today? How have you seen God's hand in pruning your life to bear more fruit?

_____

_____

_____

the Wound

"Hardship often prepares an ordinary person for an
extraordinary destiny."
—C.S. LEWIS[24]

I'm made for hardship; I can feel it in my code. I came prepared for
trouble, my clamping muscles, the fluid built up within me ready to
repair tears in my flesh. It's weird too, like someone made me able to
withstand the turbulent tides and foes who have it in for me. And it's
a good thing, because I've been hit, and hit hard. I don't know what is
happening in me now, alarms are going off and I don't recognize myself
anymore. Everything in me feels swollen, tight, off, and in spite of the
fluid rushing to the cut, it isn't going away. If anything, it seems to be
getting worse, just duller. Like the pain is getting bigger, more spread
out, but less intense. But I don't know a better way of surviving at this
point, I'm just doing what I know to do.

I'm trying to stop the pain.

And the worst part is, I hate being here now. Living. Nothing feels
right anymore, the deep is dark and scary, and all I can think about is
this ugly place in me. Nothing appears to have changed on the outside,

all seems normal for everyone else; but for me, I feel damaged and dirty. And there's nothing I can do about it.

I was a good student in elementary school, one of the best really. I excelled in my studies without much effort and was loved by all the teachers and staff. I had friends who liked me, who wanted me around because I was funny. I had meals regularly, rode my bike after school, had a bed of my own and spent weekly time with grandparents who gave me lots of love and attention.

You would never know that inside I was carrying deep shame, guilt, anger and fear. Even though what had happened to me as a child was not my fault, and gave no cause for me to feel guilt, I internalized the guilt and shame of the offenders as my own. I didn't know how to carry sadness without wearing shame too. No one knew I felt dirty, or that much of my over-achieving and humor was my feeble attempt to rid myself of the disgust I felt toward myself. How could they know? I didn't even know.

Well, the kids I beat up probably had a hint.

We lived in a trailer park in the shape of a figure eight, with our house on the street where the circles touched. I had a couple of neighbor friends and, as many kids do, we shared an after-school pastime. First, always, we would tear into our homes, strip off our backpacks, tell whoever was there the 10 second highlight of the day, then mount our bikes and transform into wild explorers discovering the great wide unknown of that full figure eight. I felt free on my bike. Wind whipping my hair and pressing my shirt against my stomach, never did I feel so light than when I pumped those pedals on that lavender and gray Huffy 10-speed. My legs felt strong and lean and didn't rub together like when I ran. The sound of asphalt scraping underneath me only told me how fast I could ride, it said nothing about my weight. On a bike, I forgot how much I didn't like my body. In fact, all I could think about was how amazing it felt to be alive.

One day though, one of the neighbor friends came running to my house crying before I could meet her on the street on my wheels. Diamond was a blonde, sweet and delicate child. She reminded me of those Precious Moments dolls with big pear-shaped eyes that hung a little low and sad. She had been riding her bike around the top circle and was making her way down my street to the bottom circle, when a teenage mean girl came out and pushed her off. Then she did the same to Diamond's brother. It was shocking. Nothing bad ever happened to us on our bikes, minus a scraped knee here or there. So many places felt unsafe to me as a child, but not when I was on my bike. And I wasn't about to lose that too.

I told Diamond to go back to her home and take her brother with her. I'd see her later. I went back inside and felt adrenaline coursing through my young body. I wasn't thinking about anyone or anything except that mean girl and my friends and our bike adventures. This girl, "Alicia" represented more to me than I understood at the time, but I was tired of being a victim. So I hatched a plan.

My dad was adding onto our front porch, creating a little deck with steps and storage underneath. We had lots of wood pieces tossed underneath from the scraps, so I took one. I took a plank of 2 x 4 wood and lodged it down the back of my pants to hold it against my back. I could feel the rawness scratching my skin and figured a splinter was worth it to have our freedom back in the neighborhood. With that board snuggly tucked, and anger to fuel a train, I set out to ride the eight.

I was surprised I could even hear her screen door creak open with the cattle herd stampeding in my chest. The adrenaline surged up through my chest into my throat rattling my eardrums like I was peddling through a tunnel with four lanes of traffic at rush hour. Based on her past rotten behavior toward kids on the street I fully expected her to throw me down. The seconds that passed next stretched to ten times their length as I came to a hockey stop, lowered and planted my feet squarely on the crumbling asphalt, drew my board from my pants and swung wide.

She was right up on me when I walloped her to the ground.

I must have made contact with her face, or she landed on it, because I noticed her hand go to her cheek as she screamed and ran inside. I can't be sure because I didn't stick around to learn the details! I pedaled so fast it was as if a tornado swept me up and spit me out at my house. I threw the board under the porch, scrambled up tripping back to my room and then cried my eyes out. I was both proud of myself and ashamed of myself all at once. I waited for the sound of sirens to come for me. Surely I was going to jail for life. The sirens never sounded though. In fact, later that day I went outside and there were no sounds on our street at all. I went to Diamond's house and confessed; my conscience couldn't carry the load. I told her I thought we might be safe to ride again, but I'd wait a day to be sure. Oh, and that I hoped she'd write to me in jail. The next day I surveyed the roads and rode the eight. We never had trouble on our bikes again.

Occasionally years later I'd see Alicia waiting for her bus, and eventually I felt bad for her. Even I knew then that people who hurt you are themselves hurting. She and I probably had more in common than we thought. She had just chosen that day to use her hurt to cause pain for evil, while I used mine to keep bike riding safe for all.

But I didn't always use my emotional fuel for just causes, and that led to deeper shame. I just couldn't keep "good" up all the time. No one could see the shame I was carrying, the fear, anger and pain. But that's the mystery with a cut. The cut itself is not necessarily the worst harm. Sure, it is a harm, but the greater harm is the message, or messages, it leaves behind. The message behind the cut can go deep like an infection that continues to work against you long after the cutting is over.

*"For I will restore health to you and heal you of your wounds,'
declares the Lord, 'Because they called you an outcast saying...
No one seeks her.'"*

—JEREMIAH 30:17

Eve believed a lie, and made a decision based on that mistruth. This was the cut, and while it was painful to her and Adam, and all of us as a result, the wound went deeper yet. The wound was that her nakedness, her truest self, was bad, wrong, dirty, and needed to be covered. The wound was that God was angry at her, that she needed to hide herself, and mostly from Him.

> "...and Adam and his wife hid themselves from the presence of the LORD God among the trees of the garden."[25]

Eve and Adam's choice changed everything for humanity. Sin came in the front door and shame snuck in the back. Even then though, God set out a redemption plan and promised Eve that her seed would bruise the heel of the deceiver. She must have heard God clearly on this point, because when she bore Cain she said, "I have acquired a man from the LORD."[26] Imagine her hope brimming, thinking that this must be what God was talking about, her seed was a child who would make the mess they were in all better again. Cain wasn't the seed God was talking about though. The work of sin and shame would continue to regenerate, but through a seed of a different nature.

Cain's story is a sad one. First, we find him in conflict because he was trying to worship God on his own terms, keeping the best for himself. Rather than call it what it was and do the right thing, he chose to kill his only brother who was making him look bad. His choice brought blood on the earth and ended with his exile from God's presence. God's generous mercy allowed for Cain to live and inhabit a land without fear of being murdered for his wickedness, but his sin seed was already rooting and was about to reproduce. It wasn't long before Cain formed a city and his descendants became a highly industrialized civilization. The Caininic civilization grew in number and technological advancement. Remember the brilliance of God's first created human minds, and the incredibly long life-span? The society pre-Flood was likely much more developed than we ever give them credit for. They weren't the Neanderthals depicted in evolutionary stories. In fact, God's creation moves from perfect down to decay because of sin on the earth. Any evidence of animalistic civilization is better attributed to the degenerative way of humanity than the pure beginning of it. As soon as humanity has time to multiply, as did Cain, immediately we see it move toward colonization and industry. But even with all the blessings of near-perfect DNA and relatively limitless freedom, the compromised nature of humanity moves also toward destruction. The pre-Flood society on the earth was later described as "corrupt before God, and… filled with violence…for all flesh had corrupted their way on the earth."[27] Murder was rampant, there was nothing left that was good, though God saved a remnant through Noah's family and a host of animals. The wound from the first cut in the Garden was festering on the earth until the land could bear it no longer and judgment washed in as a Flood.

Still, God cared for His humanity, and had a redemption plan in place.

Eve's heartache was unimaginable, first the grief of sin, but then the weight of shame, the loss of two sons and a dream of forever washed away. The clothing made from a sacrifice provided a pardon for her sin, but what was she to do with the shame that likely haunted her relentlessly as she buried her one son and said good-bye to the other? "If only I had never believed that lie…"

In her book *Released from Shame* Dr. Sandra Wilson explains three kinds of shame we experience in our progressive journey as soul-bearers. The first shame is in our youthfulness, a "biological shame", a realization that we are small and not grown yet. I can see this first shame in my daughter, who cries when she discovers she is "too little" for certain rides. It's an awareness of what we are not, and this tempts us to believe that this gap is a fatal flaw in us. That we are *wrong* because of what we are not. This shame resolves for most of us by the simple remedy of actually growing up. We just get bigger, usually.

A second shame, which she calls a "Biblical shame" arises though when we realize we are not perfect, that there is perfect (God), but we are not Him. For those of us who believe God's Word and trust in Jesus as the promised Messiah who absolves all our sins through His blood sacrifice, we find the gap between our imperfection and God's perfection bridged. We are reconciled with the perfect God through Christ's death and resurrection, and our perfection is based on Jesus' unchanging perfection. For those though who do not trust in Jesus as the Messiah, this gap continues to haunt them and striving to be "good enough" is their life effort to quiet this shame. The third shame Dr. Wilson describes is one many Christians overlook and underestimate, and I believe it is what keeps most of us from sharing our stories and investing in the lives of others in our communities. This shame, or "binding shame" as she puts it, is one we carry in our souls related to unresolved pain from wounds in our lives. Naturally, they can vary from extreme emotional pains related to sexual abuse to nagging struggles with insecurities. What is true of all of us with binding shame though, is that our hope is found in discovering God's truth and exchanging this for the lies woven into our belief system.[28]

Binding shame is released when we experience truth, because truth sets us free. This is why Jesus "is the answer"—Jesus is the "Word" and the Word of God is truth. Freedom is what we want, so truth is what we need, and Jesus has it and is it for us.

God immediately dealt with the offense of sin in the garden and unfolded His next step in a redemption plan for our forefather and foremother, which included a curse on the deceiver as well as tunics to cover their nakedness. God couldn't just tell them, "Oh don't let the nakedness bother you, you look great, let it go." The shame was inside them, not an external insecurity. They were aware of darkness and nothing could keep them from the distraction of this awareness. There was no un-learning, they had to move forward with a new normal. Garments weren't God's concern then, nor were they when He called the people of Israel to repent of their rejection:

> "...'Turn to Me with all your heart, with fasting, with weeping, and with mourning'...so rend your heart, and not your garments..."[29]

Sin breaks the heart of God, and this is the greater wounding than us breaking His rules. He loved Adam and Eve, still does, and no doubt He grieved the loss of perfect joy they once had with Him in that garden. Even more devastating is that God grieved the burden placed on their relationship because of the shame that sent them into hiding away from Him.

Shame may come in words, but shame doesn't get the last one. God always has the final word on every matter.

Before God sent His solution for sin and shame, His Son Jesus, He told His people shame had an end. In spite of Israel's constant rejection and abandonment, God covenanted with Abraham to make his descendants a nation, give them a land and establish for them a government, where Jesus would be the perfect King. This unlikely race of people would be the beneficiaries of the most shocking and wide display of God's grace because His promise was His promise. He has been faithful to make and sustain the people of Israel as a nation. He has been bringing them back to the land promised to them in increasing number over the last several decades, and a government will be set in place with Christ returning to reign as King.

> "...You shall eat in plenty and be satisfied, and praise the name of the Lord your God, who has dealt wondrously with you; and My people shall never be put to shame. Then you shall know that I am in the midst of Israel; I am the LORD your God and there is no other. My people shall never be put to shame."[30]

Israel has no doubt *felt* shame in her history. Attacked relentlessly since her inception by foreign invaders, hated and reviled by world leaders, strategically stalked and systematically demoralized and murdered in historic accounts, Israel's existence today is proof of God's grace and sovereign work among humanity. She should not be here today, but she is, and she has a future in God's story.

And the Church, comprised of Gentiles who before Christ were without hope of being folded into God's family, now have hope of a future with God. We are God's people by faith in Christ alone, the descendants of Abraham by faith. We have promises as co-heirs with Christ, inheriting all that belongs to Him.

However, the wound of shame will continue on for eternity too, just not for us. The ones who will bear shame will be the ones who did not put their trust in Christ to bear it for them.

> "...they are the enemies of the cross of Christ: whose end is destruction, who god is their belly, and whose glory is in their shame—who set their mind on earthly things."[31]

But what of Eve's hope? How did her story turn? Eve amazingly never gave up hope in spite of Cain's rebellion and Abel's death. When it seemed all hope was lost, when it looked like the answer to the mess and the hope of redemption and restoration was buried, Eve believed God. We see her clinging to His promise of redemption in the name she gave her third born, but "oldest son" Seth. His name means, "For God has appointed another seed for me instead of Abel whom Cain killed."[32] Eve is unfairly regarded with disdain often, yet even after suffering the worst trauma to hit earth, and after suffering unimaginable heartbreak as a parent this pioneer of womanhood put her hope in God's redemption power. I don't know when Eve died, I know Adam walked the same earth as Noah's dad, Lamech. Another 720 years, and Adam could have boarded the ark himself. So perhaps God gave Eve a vision of what would come from her seed, that Seth would go on to walk with God, and generations later a Messiah would redeem the curse. Maybe she saw her seed triumph over her sin in the face of Seth. If she didn't see it then, I believe she sees it now and is cheering her progeny along to the finish line!

Hope abounds for the wounded in this life. Our hope is found in the real person of Jesus Christ, the seed of Adam and Eve, the Son of God, Mary and Joseph. He fulfills Old Testament prophecies, provides for our sin problem, removes our shame through His reconciliation between God and us, and sets us free from the deceptive messages that work to destroy us as we renew our minds in His truth.

So really, what cut can truly harm us, the ones who belong to God? The words that lodge in us through cuts meant for our harm are used for our good as they draw us closer to the Word that heals.

MY REDEMPTION STORY

There were clear messages playing on repeat in my mind, festering wounds from my cuts. As a result of my first cut, my inherited nature as a descendant of Adam and Eve, I had a natural bent to doing what was not good for me, choosing what was evil over what was good like we see every child do naturally. The other childhood exposures to evil then only served to reinforce a deep sense of wrongness within me, a sense that I was dirty. And it wasn't only the evil I was exposed to, but the evil I chose to do in response to the anger and pain I felt inside. Not all of my abuses were motivated by a sense of "street justice", sometimes I was just angry and took it out on others. Daily though, in mental and physical ways, I abused my body in order to deaden the constant sensation of inner pain.

Other messages brought confusion and shame as well, and one was so dark, I buried it so deep even I didn't really notice it for years. The message was that I was a mistake, I wasn't good at being a girl, in fact, I wasn't even a girl. I was a boy. I was both uncomfortable in my feminine body and at the same time didn't think I looked as feminine as other girls I knew. I didn't know how to use make-up well, my hair was cut short at a young age, my voice and personality were both loud and deep, I was bigger than the boys in my class and was terrified of unwanted attention toward my body by boys or men. I preferred the safety of girl friendships and would often stand as a protector of them against the mean things boys would say and do, often incurring their mean words aimed at me instead. I'll share more about how God worked in this message later, but this was how I felt at this point in my life.

In response to these scary messages, the wound deceived me by bringing me more messages with different harms of their own, offering false hope and the promise of cleansing. I believed I would be worth something if I championed a cause, so in elementary school I started advocating for certain social justice issues, and even ended up on the news for standing out against "new age" practices being imposed on us as students. While I sincerely believed at a young age that some things were worth speaking out against, I was driven by a desire to earn my existence.

I also believed I needed to perform until there was praise, so I joined every club or activity and performed until I heard clapping. I was awarded "Best All Around" in the 5th grade. It was the award to trump all awards. But as good as that felt, it only lasted until I got home and faced a quiet summer home, often by myself. I determined to do whatever I had to do to stay busy performing so I never felt that inner turmoil. I quickly joined the band, and ironically chose the loudest and biggest instrument: the tuba.

In spite of the heavy weight of the tuba, I believed I needed to be light and easy-going. I never wanted to demand too much in friendship or be a burden to my authorities, so I kept my needs to myself and let private tears and public humor become my inadequate emotional outlets. I also believed being thin meant I would be more accepted, good, and feminine somehow. I started restrictive dieting around age 10 and by high school I was bound in disordered eating. I used food binges to numb the unresolved grief and then extreme exercise or deprivation to manage the weight gain and guilt. I didn't know how to relate to food in a healthy way, it was feast or famine.

I also believed I needed a boyfriend. I thought if I was in a relationship with someone I could validate my sense of womanhood. Being single was a silence my soul couldn't handle for long lest someone see in me what I feared was true. I started dating in middle school and learned quickly that the emotional high of infatuation helped hide pain too. But break ups were another story. To avoid the pain of breaking up I just learned how to repress any negative emotions that stirred up in relationship with others. I thought no one would leave me again if I stayed sweet and airy like cotton candy.

Anger over feeling helpless against predators, fear over being a victim again, and the pain of having wounds with unmet needs drove me to defend and protect others from bullies and oppressors. At the same time, shame drove me to fight a cause at all times, to be a savior in order to make myself worth something, anything. And deep down, I knew...I was the one who was in need of a savior. And soon.

I was in law school when I finally faced one of the deepest wounds from my childhood cuts. It was during a weekend in Orlando where I was by myself attending a Christian women's conference. I didn't really want to go, especially by myself, but I was drawn to it because of the title: "Destined by Design". I didn't know exactly what would be discussed but I thought about both my design and destiny often. When I would think of myself I never thought about my femaleness first. I thought in terms of talents and gifts and figured the conference might help me figure out what I was doing with my life. Even though I was in law school, I still didn't know what I wanted to be when I grew up, I had interests that seemed to run in every direction. I had never been to an all-women's conference before, so I kept my expectations for enjoying it low and sat near the back in case I needed to bolt out.

As I listened to the women share, I couldn't imagine they could relate to what I had been through, or how I felt. None of them seemed to be as backwards as I felt when it came to being a woman. I especially started to tune out when one woman in particular stepped up to share during the last session of the night. As she walked up the steps I took in messages from what I saw of her: blonde hair flowing, exquisite make-up, shapely nails, sculpted arms, thin waist and model-like legs draped in a stylish feminine dress. Her image pronounced perfection on the stage and I concluded we lived worlds apart. But then she opened her mouth and the words that came out shattered the image being projected. As she shared her story of insecurity, of rejection and abandonment, of fear and shame, and of her own infidelity against her pastor husband that resulted in her bearing another man's child, she looked entirely different to me. She wept telling of her husband's forgiveness, of God's grace and acceptance and of her own journey to understand for the first time God's love for her and her place in His heart. Through her vulnerability a bridge was crafted for our shared humanity to connect across. Her story endeared me to her, yes. But more than that her story stirred up a curiosity in me to know God the way she knew Him. I hadn't experienced Him this way yet and wondered who this God is who is so kind and forgiving even to *wild* women?

She shared how God had released her from bondage to lies about her worth, her sexuality, and her identity. As she spoke God's Word went out and it flooded hard ground deep in my heart until something began to release in me. After that session I was too stirred to sleep. I stayed up all night long writing with Jesus, recounting my journey to Him (as if He didn't know it!) and listening to His words back to me. The messages that had sunk low from the cuts began to bubble to the surface of my mind. Messages like *I'm a boy.* Some came up through chokes; as if they were being pried off an internal organ. Once they were out though, it was as if we had something to work with between God and I. The message would sit on the paper in script and I would ask Him if it was true. I had a lot of messages written down about who I believed I was, it was a long night through some painful memories. When the sun came up though, my feminine soul rose with it. I believed God. I believed He made me. I believed He saw me in a womb and formed my inward parts. I believed He made me female regardless of how "girlie" I did or didn't feel.

That small faith opened a new door in my mind and it was as if I had permission to enjoy being a girl. The timing was perfect, or the worst if you look at it from the perspective of my budget. We were within walking distance of an outlet shopping center and it seemed like the right time to get some new clothes. At that time my wardrobe consisted of baggy jeans, sweatshirts and mostly dark colors with a few exceptions. Before I returned home I was wearing white jeans, a soft pink sweater and shimmering lip gloss. My mom had begged and pleaded with me for years to wear pastels, but I would have nothing of it. One night with Jesus though and I left with a car loaded down with nothing but pastels! My feminine style has evolved since that weekend, my wardrobe carries every color today, but the permission to be a woman and enjoy it has never left me. God did for me what I could never do. He met me in my wound and brought truth that set me free to be who He created me to be, and He does it every day for those who seek Him.

DISCUSSION QUESTIONS
5—THE WOUND

YOUR REDEMPTION STORY

What messages have you believed about who you are, who God is and how He sees you?

_____

_____

_____

How did these messages play out in your life?

_____

_____

_____

OTHER REDEMPTIVE STORIES

How do you see lies about who you are still causing you trouble?

_____

_____

_____

Share one wound that persists, and how you treat it. If you've turned to God with it, what has He done for you?

_____

_____

_____

the Nacre

"Mental pain is less dramatic than physical pain, but it is more common and also more hard to bear. The frequent attempt to conceal mental pain increases the burden: it is easier to say "My tooth is aching" than to say "My heart is broken."

—C.S. LEWIS[33]

After the cuts I became a collector, but not of pretty things. In the only way I knew how, I collected layers, liquid at first, then hardened layers to try to deaden the intensity of the pain throbbing in my tender tissue. I didn't set out to "burden myself" in a greater way, I just tried the next thing to feel better. And for a little while, the layering did feel better! When things get quiet and still, I can feel the ache deep down and an alarm sounds releasing this soothing elixir to do its mind-numbing job. Layer after layer, my nature releases this flow to the place of my tear, a constant balm barricading me away from my wound. Honestly, I don't know if I'd make it if I felt the fullness of my cut, but the layers are thickening now and I find a new problem before me. My new normal is a co-existence with this growing burden inside me, and I'm running out of space to breathe. It's been months now, even years since I first felt a cut, but I don't see any hope of the pain ending. At the same time, I don't know how to stop myself from layering either...who can save me from this body of death?

The way we react to our pain as a child is largely instinctive. Our eyes blink when debris flies inside, our body raises its temperature to fight off infection, our skin sends blood to form a scab when we are cut. But when we are cut in our soul, when the pain is mental or emotional, we react in ways that may alleviate pain immediately, but could create a bigger burden for us if the measures are simply pain avoidant, not restorative. Coupled with messages of shame, infection can set in to our soul so that our external comforts (food, drugs, alcohol, illicit sex...), only soothe us at the surface of our pain. The initial infection, however, continues to work in us a deeper harm.

As a child, there is no way to know that what you are doing is in response to an emotional or spiritual wound, unless your parents are pastors or therapists and bedtime prayers are counseling sessions. Even then, the ability to understand the anatomy of your soul comes much later in development, if it is even developed at all.

I want to reiterate here, I'm not a psychiatrist, or a licensed counselor. Neither am I a theologian. I'm a lawyer by trade, a writer because it helps me understand life, and a speaker because I communicate with words and hands that won't stay by my side. This book is not a therapeutic aid for emotional healing per se, though it does contain truth from God's Word, which is the ultimate source of our healing. I'm just a woman with a redemption story, often a lover of myself but growing in my love for God. This book is my redemption story, plus some other redemptive stories in my life along with questions to guide you in telling your own stories. If you haven't been doing so already maybe this book will start you on a journey of processing the events in your life in a relatively healthy way. I say "relatively" because we are always working through our stories, at least to some degree.

I used to think when I became an adult I would just be "healthy" emotionally because I was a Christian. We become children in God's family the moment we put our trust in Jesus for our sins, so our biggest human problem is resolved by faith alone instantly. But we don't arrive at emotional health in an instant. There have been many times when I felt as if I was moving backwards in my maturing journey. I've done all the right things, taken all the best steps to make the wisest choices, and yet I feel heavy, lost and unsure of just about everything. My feelings can betray me. My emotions can masquerade themselves as if real injuries are taking place when they may not be in fact happening. One day I see what God says and believe it. I stand confidently in who I am and make decisions like I am the boss of my mind. Those days are paradise! Then a tide changes, a mysterious current pulls me under and I'm clamoring to find shoreline. The change in my emotions can come quickly and from out of nowhere. I am tempted to believe I'm going backwards and will never change. I grow less hopeful of ever being better than I am. The truth is our emotions are under the sway of the same curse as the beach. With its majesty also comes its tumult. Wisdom in God's Word provides the solid ground I need when my emotions sway. All other ground is sinking sand.

It is wise for me to root deeply and daily in God's Word so I know truth and am not as vulnerable to my fleeting feelings. It is also wise for me to pay attention and create wider space in my schedule for my soul to rest on days I know will feel overwhelming. It is not unhealthy for me to feel negative emotions; it is unhealthy for me to never feel them at all. If my schedule lacks space in my days to actually feel emotions and give my over-stimulated soul a rest, the emotions will pressurize. One of the greatest discoveries I made in my journey with God is that feeling pain can be the healthiest thing for me, just as feeling heat on a stove protects me from greater harm. Emotional pain can be a warning that I'm believing lies or making choices out of fear. I could be avoiding pain God is wanting to surface because that pain will protect me from a greater pain. It could also be accumulated grief from living in a world filled with sorrow, and my soul just needs to empty out to make room for hope again. This life is hard, on all of us.

We give our cars room to adjust and leak and refresh every 3000 miles, and yet we wear the tread out on our souls for decades before taking them off the road for a full check-up. Many Christians may be wondering why they aren't growing or having a wider impact, when it could be that they are neglecting their real emotional needs by hiding behind spiritual personalities or activities. Pastor and author Peter Scazzero states that, "… the spirituality of most current discipleship models often only add[s] an additional protective layer against people growing up emotionally."[34] Making space to grieve, to mourn, to weep before God when the soul is calling for it, could be the release you need to bring you into a new season of influence, or at least a deeper soul rest. The resulting empathy we come away with for others suffering is vastly beneficial as well, and binds us closer to our fellow humans, which is never a bad thing.

Of course, there are cases where deep healing has yet to begin. Sometimes medication and supervision is needed to best care for our soul and body's needs. There is no shame in this journey either, none that is appropriate at least. In fact, I have great admiration for women when I hear they are taking brave steps to move toward emotional health. The first steps can feel like failure, like we should have been able to figure this "life thing" out without someone else's help. Yet God said it wasn't good for a perfect human in a perfect world to be alone. If the first human needed a helper, why do we let shame harass us when we need the same support?

"To what will you look for help if you will not look to that which is stronger than yourself?"

—C.S. LEWIS[35]

To make matters more difficult, our emotional healing journey is not a straight route. It's not that we don't know where to find help. Biblical counselors are relatively easy to find these days in our country. But the challenge is found in the layers we have accumulated over the years: the ways we have met our own needs for comfort, security and approval. These include the paths we have let our minds run down defining our identity in ways that are misaligned with truth. Over time we have learned ways to live that are not actually helping us move toward who we are destined to become. Just as the oyster reacts to her pain with liquid-then-hardening self-protective layers called nacre, we too form a kind of nacre. We depend on our own unique blend of survival efforts that help us live a high-functioning pain-centered life. We get neurological rewards for blocking pain so we learn to repeat the behavior to get more rewards. It's not long before we find ourselves stuck literally in a rut wanting to be someone else with no clear path how to get there. The reality is we've been layering over pain for years doing the best we can to survive, it is unrealistic to expect complete healing to come in an instant!

Even after we accept the need to feel pain in our lives, it is still not so simple to let go of the destructive habits that have formed our nacre. We will not let go of supports, regardless of how convinced we are of their harm to us, until we have another support to cling to in exchange. The journey of emotional healing then is connected to our spiritual healing because we are learning to trust that God is committed to our souls and our bodies. We will not let go of what offers us immediate comfort, even if it is binding us deeper in shame, unless we know God has something better for us. And trust takes time to build. It is not an overnight transfer from a god to the God. There is good news though. While it will take time to learn new paths, with each new choice to believe truth we get a little freer because the truth sets us free! A little freer today is better than completely stuck yesterday, especially when there is hope of being even freer in the future. When we practice trusting God to help us, even in the tiniest ways, we discover He is faithful. We will grow in our experience of emotional health as we learn to trust God, and we may even experience greater joy in our physical health too if we have been locked up in stress responses. Regardless of our measure of health in this life though, emotional or physical, God will be faithful to redeem every tear and restore every wounded place in the eternal life we are moving into soon. Why not seek as much of it here though as we can?

Another reason I highly recommend therapeutic specialists or restoration fellowships like Celebrate Recovery or Regeneration, is because God didn't design us to live, or heal, in isolation. In his book *Anatomy of the Soul*, Dr. Curt Thompson explains a difference between *knowing* and *being known*.

> "Knowing…is an activity that involves a primary subject (or person) thinking, feeling, or acting while separated from the idea, object, or person…"[36]

Knowing about something and sharing that knowledge with another person can still keep people separated. In that separation, hidden places of brokenness remain so. But being known requires a deeper connection that allows for a release into healing:

> "To be known means that you allow your shame and guilt to be exposed—in order for them to be healed."[37]

It isn't enough to grieve a pain, or even journal it and process it with God. We need the exchange of story and words with another person. When we live in community, it is an easy thing to celebrate in that community, but we need to grieve and heal in community as well. Aligning our inner life with our communal life is our life-long aim for emotional health and peace, being first fully accepted by God through Christ, and then becoming fully ourselves before God and others.

"Then the eyes of both of them were opened, and they knew that they were naked; and they sewed fig leaves together and made themselves loin coverings."

—GENESIS 3:1-7

Adam and Eve knew how to layer. We come by it honestly.

The irritant slipped deception into the soft inner belly of innocence in humanity. A cut was made with the prick of doubt in God's Word and a willful choice to act on it. The wound set in and shame went deep. Humanity's response to God, after the wound of shame, was to hide. They didn't hide from one another, or the irritant, but from holiness. Deep down they knew they were not what they once were. They had been changed. Unholy could not stand bare before holy, so they tried to make a way for themselves. But their best efforts amounted to a leaf. A leaf was essentially all the unholy had to hold up before a holy God who knew them, knew what happened, and pursued them still. They layered over their pain, shame and guilt. They hid from God, blamed each other and feared God's anger at them.

Meanwhile, God never said He was angry. God never told them to cover their nakedness. God never asked them to hide. Instructions were coming from another place, a source now within them that wasn't present before sin. They projected their shame onto God when He had nothing to do with any of it. His only role in the scene was being the One who knew everything and yet still pursued them.

It wasn't until after the story unfolded, after fault was found with the irritant for his sabotage, after Adam and Eve had to face God and themselves in truth, that consequences were addressed. Even then, and at the same time, a redemption plan was set into motion.

To the woman, reproduction was touched. She received the ability to live and give life from Adam and God, but this would be mixed with difficulties now.

To the man, the land was touched. He received the ability to walk and work from the ground and God, but labor would be hard and would now end in death.

But God was already prepared to do for Adam and Eve what they were incapable of doing for themselves. He provided the sacrifice for their sins. He was the first to slay His own creation for the sake of humanity's wrong doing. He took life from one of His animals then made tunics of the skin to cover the shame of His people. From the first sin to the last, life-blood was the only adequate exchange for sin, and the only bridge between the unholy and the Holy. God's nacre, His layering for His people, was pure and righteous and is the nacre we all need to cover our sin wounds so we can stand before Him. Whatever else we may bring with us, when we come out of hiding before God, is worthless.

We may as well bring a leaf.

MY REDEMPTION STORY

My nacre was comprised of a variety of efforts to numb pain I didn't know how else to manage as a child. The messages haunting me were heavy with shame, guilt and fear. At times I felt completely overwhelmed emotionally, especially when my hormones ramped up in my pre-teen years. I coped with the emotional pain largely in secret, just not understanding myself and not wanting others to know what I was thinking or what I had experienced. In elementary school I formed a hard-shell personality as a funny, but tough girl. It helped that I was bigger than the other students, even the boys. I was always the first pick for tug-of-war and last pick for relay races. I spent as much time under the tree on the P.E. field for getting into fights with boys than I did on the pavement playing foursquare. If I was attacked, I attacked back, with words or fists. Otherwise I'd charm with my humor to keep people happy, so they wouldn't attack or reject me. At home I'd use food to calm my anxiety built up after a day of self-protection and masking insecurities. After school I'd sneak extra snacks, and after dinner I'd binge on leftovers as I cleaned the dishes. Food was the only "drug" I had access to, and it provided the quick rush of pleasure and distraction that I was desperate to feel. It helped that food was also used by others in my family as well, so it was joked about and accepted as a reasonable comfort for emotional needs. But the guilt remained with me, and even grew as I binged on food in secret. With it came heaping shame too, as my body stretched out and kids said cruel things. My nacre only grew thicker as my emotional pain increased, begging for relief with more food. The only way out I saw was to start deprivation dieting, and/or purging through induced vomiting or excessive exercise. Self was my god, appearance meant everything if I didn't want to feel the pain of rejection or abandonment. Being a "good kid" with no problems was essential if I was going to be worth anything. But my pants told the real story; we were both bursting at the seams and something needed to give.

At this point in my redemption story, I hadn't yet heard the Gospel, that would come later. I was devoted to food as my comforter and faithful friend through hard times. But even years later, after trusting in Jesus and learning to walk with Him a little better, food continued to hold a high place in my soul. Without a doubt, one of the most refining challenges in my life has been the slow release of my unhealthy dependency on food for my emotional needs. I have other areas too, to be sure, but this one is unavoidable because we have to eat! And regularly! My nacre not only produced invisible self-protecting layers that kept my real self hidden for years; I also formed layers of rounded-ness around my hips and thighs for all to see! Shame continued to knock on my door, bullying me with taunts like, "Why can't you overcome this? It's just food!" or "If you really loved God you would stop overeating". I wasn't just harming my body, or hiding my emotions, or neglecting my soul; but now I believed I was being a "bad Christian" too. Some family members would praise me when I'd "succeed" at weight loss, then silently look me up and down casting judgment when it inevitably returned. Even though I was a Christian, I still believed my worth was tied to my ability to maintain a perfect appearance, and at times that my womanhood was still tied to my weight.

In my early 20s I cried out to God for help. I was stuck. He had already proven Himself faithful in many ways through college, so my trust in Him had grown enough that I was ready to try trusting Him with my food bondage too. I expected He would take me back to deprivation dieting and tell me to "try harder". Though I did get impatient at times and jumped into severely restrictive eating patterns to get results faster, what God kept drawing me to was His love. In the night when I'd cry in exhaustion from all my efforts to lose weight He'd whisper in His Word messages of love. He'd show me the mercy and compassion of Christ toward women when He walked the dust of this earth. I saw His presence and provision for Israel and even Gentiles in the Old Testament. God delivered me out of fad deprivation eating cycles around age 25, and it felt like living in the wilderness as I depended on Him to provide for my hunger needs physically and emotionally, one day at a time. But it wasn't just Him and I on the journey. He brought encouraging friends who spoke wisdom into how to nourish both my body and soul, and as I learned more about His love for me, I was better able to practice showing this same love to myself. I could relate to Israel's experience with God. After an exhausting season of worshipping pagan gods that left her confused, empty and starved, she found hope for the comfort she longed for in the restoring love of God who spoke to her:

> ...behold, I will allure her, will bring her into the wilderness, and speak comfort to her..."[38]

Now, I'm no robot. I am *still* learning how to enjoy food for the pleasure and fuel it provides my body. I'm also learning to eat within boundaries that are wise for my unique body and season without becoming obsessed with rules. And I am *still* learning how to care for my soul well, identifying my emotional needs and meeting them in more appropriate ways. I may struggle against temptations to use food to hide my soul for the rest of my life on this red clay earth, but I know the One who will guide me back to the path and He doesn't come with a whip, but with words to heal me. I have learned that when I get out of rhythm with my eating, that my problem is not caloric so much as with my love.

> *"To love at all is to be vulnerable. Love anything and your heart will be wrung and possibly broken. If you want to make sure of keeping it intact you must give it to no one, not even an animal. Wrap it carefully round with hobbies and little luxuries; avoid all entanglements. Lock it up safe in the casket or coffin of your selfishness. But in that casket, safe, dark, motionless, airless, it will change. It will not be broken; it will become unbreakable, impenetrable, irredeemable.*
>
> *To love is to be vulnerable."*

> — C.S. LEWIS[39]

Now I know it won't be calorie counting that saves me from my worship of food, but the love of God that first saved me. First always I turn to a person, not a scale. I remember how loved I am, how secure I am in that love, how safe and accepted I am in that love, and how delighted God is in me just as I am right there in that place. In that loved place I can be vulnerable again, needy, and then I can receive God's gentle untangling of me from the food or the image I am chasing. The next step toward freedom becomes a little clearer, and a companion comes to mind so I don't step forward alone. It isn't easy, it is battle. There is death and mess when we abandon a false god to choose to worship the One God, but God's love is more powerful than any nacre we form in our souls.

And there's more good news.

Even with this nacre, this messy and inadequate way we respond to our pain that creates greater burden in our lives, we'll see how even all this is something God can redeem for His praise and fame.

Again, shame never gets the last word on those who are rescued by God.

DISCUSSION QUESTIONS
6—THE NACRE

YOUR REDEMPTION STORY

Describe the ways you've tried to bridge the gap between you and a holy God: perfection, achievement, being a good person, following spiritual rules, etc..

_____

_____

_____

How did you respond to pain triggers in your life? How did that work out for you?

_____

_____

OTHER REDEMPTIVE STORIES

Even with the abundant resources found in God's Holy Spirit, in prayer, in God's Word and in the fellowship of other believers, we still react to pain in inadequate ways. What does this look like for you? What are the conditions that make you most vulnerable to acting out in old self-protective ways that don't fit your new identity in Christ?

_____

_____

_____

What next step are you willing to take to begin responding in new ways to that pain?

_____

_____

_____

your Formation story

{Now it's your turn, make this space your own!}

Before I put my trust in Christ to forgive me of my sin, I was separated from God and nothing I did or ever could do would be enough to make things right between Him and I.

"...for all have sinned and fall short of the glory of God."

—ROMANS 3:23

Growing up ...

I believed this about God:

_____

I believed this about Jesus:

_____

I believed this about the Holy Spirit:

_____

I believed this about sin:

_____

I believed this about myself:

_____

I believed this about life after death:

_____

I responded to pain in my life by:

_____

_____

When I knew what I did was wrong I would:

_____

_____

How else would you characterize the condition of your soul before Jesus made you His own? If you'd like to add more to your formation story, do so here!

_____

_____

_____

_____

_____

_____

the Retrieval

7

the Dive

"Again, the kingdom of heaven is like unto a merchant man,
seeking goodly pearls: Who, when he had found one pearl of
great price, went and sold all that he had, and bought it."
—MATTHEW 13:45-46

I could hardly stand my life. I tried so hard to be better than I was, but
nothing I did could layer over the wound enough to make the pain stop.
If anything, I just felt worse as I continued to swell within, the pressure
becoming almost unbearable. Then, one day, I noticed a commotion in
the waters above me. Great. More trouble, I thought. It was the shimmery
light I was once drawn too, except now I wanted nothing to do with it. I
felt dark inside, light was the last thing I wanted to be in now. I clamped
down hard to prepare for the worst and then I felt something stirring in
me. I could feel myself coming unhinged from my roots, as if the earth
was giving way and for a few moments I lost all my bearings. Was
up, down? Left, right? My familiar way of understanding the deep was
falling away beneath me as I seemed to be rising up into that mysterious
light. It wasn't that my familiar world was great, or safe or comforting
even, but it was what I knew. The unknown held unspeakable fears for

me. I trust very little now. Surely, there couldn't be a better way than what I already knew, unless, there was...

My husband owns an insurance and financial agency, and has known some of our employees for almost two decades. One of those employees has shared a lot of life with us over the years, and has become a beloved friend. He is also a lively entertainer and teller of good stories. When we host work guests, we have our friend share an especially memorable story that is so remarkable, even the Governor of Tennessee at the time recognized our friend for his heroism.

It was a beautiful crisp day, and our friend was sitting on the balcony of a local restaurant eating a meal with his family. The restaurant sits on the cliff edge of a river that rises and falls significantly, usually lying low enough to see white foam polka dotted all across the river where the waves crash about the many exposed rocks. Stately houses sit at the edge of this river as well, with boat docks and beautifully landscaped yards. But on this particular day, a young girl who lived in one of those houses must have strayed too far and underestimated the river current and was soon hurtling down the rock-studded river screaming for help. Patrons at the restaurant could hear the sound of a child's screams coming from the river, but, of all the guests that day our friend was the one who immediately jumped up and over the balcony edge into the frigid unknown. In a wild few minutes he was able to reach the girl and was able to get her to shore. Both were miraculously unharmed.

When he is asked why he jumped, or what he was thinking when he was flying through the air into the river of rocks, he says he just wanted to help her, he didn't think about it really, he hoped he wouldn't hit rock and did what he thought anyone would do to save a girl. Except not everyone would do it—or did.

Our friend didn't "have" to dive into those dangerous waters to save that girl, he had no obligation, no debt to pay, no responsibility to her. He dove because he desired her alive, to rescue her, to save her from death. He was compelled by love; whether he knew it or not, his actions expressed it.

I love this story, not just because of my friend's heroism but because of how afraid I am of unknown waters. Remember "the Deep"? To dive into dangerous water is, to me, a great demonstration of love. I can appreciate our friend's sacrifice because I know what it would cost me to choose to face unknown water, and it would probably have to be my child drowning to motivate me in love. I may not be motivated enough for another adult, or even another's child, if I'm being painfully honest.

Thankfully, our eternal future isn't dependent on my willingness to give my life for another, or for you to give your life for another. Even if we did give our lives for one another, it would never be enough to absolve us of our sin problem! There is only One who could dive into this dangerous river of humanity and rescue us, and thankfully He did.

"I will give you the treasures of darkness and hidden wealth of secret places, so that you may know that it is I, the LORD, the God of Israel, who calls you by your name."

—ISAIAH 45:3

The Bible gives us progressive revelation of God's plan for humanity and the earth. We don't learn everything in the beginning, not about God, Jesus, the Holy Spirit, not about the seas, the creatures of the air or the trees in the wilderness. We don't learn everything about Adam or Eve, or the irritant who deceived them. Even God's name is progressively expressed to us. We don't know about sin on Day 1, about sacrificial blood required to reconcile sinner with God. We don't know of God's earthly plan for a special race of people known as the Jews, and we don't know about a redemption plan for them or a salvation plan for Gentiles. Not on Day 1. The revelation of God's plan unfolds as every story naturally unfolds, one step at a time as told by the author.

But from the first tunic of skin God made for Eve and Adam, from the first shedding of blood for the first sins of humanity, God saw Jesus on a cross. This means Jesus saw Himself on a cross for us. To redeem the whole earth under this curse, only holy blood could bridge the gap between the unholy and holy. Jesus would have to shed His own holy blood and cover us with the tunic of His perfect life.

Though God sent Jesus, Jesus dove in willingly. God didn't have to push Him to earth, there was no guilt trip or debt Jesus owed to God, they were One. Jesus got up from His perfect throne, jumped into a dangerous river of humanity and not only risked His life for us, He died. He hit rock, for us. It was a death mission. And He dove in anyway.

Jesus gave it all up, to dive to earth for us. Not because of a duty, but because he sought a treasure. His motivation was not the praise of man, but a heart full of love for people who were screaming, whether we knew it or not. Just as pearl divers risk their lives to dive because they know there is treasure beneath the frigid and dangerous dark depths, Jesus saw us as His treasure, and only He could retrieve us.

Jesus had the treasure map. He knew the way because He was the way. He was not repulsed by our burdens of sin and shame, quite the opposite. He was driven by them, compelled by love to come and rescue us from the weight of it all.

We can know that whatever we are to Him, and to God, whatever value we must hold must be great if it was worth Him diving to a dusty, ungrateful, unhinging earth, just to have us as His own.

MY REDEMPTION STORY

Before I understood the Gospel, what I knew of Jesus came from Easter plays in the churches we visited. I remember shiny banners with words in Hebrew I didn't understand, Easter lilies wrapped in green foil lining the altars, and the cross. For some reason, I never struggled with the fact that God existed, and accepted that He bore an heir in human flesh to a virgin named Mary. Why I never really questioned this is perhaps just God's gift of faith for me, and I'm grateful for this faith. But beyond that, the Gospel story was all Hebrew to me. That was until one night when I was 11 years old. My mom dropped me off to hear a visiting youth pastor speak to kids. I had never done "church" without a parent before, so I was both excited and a little sick to my stomach. I could perform for others to get accepted at school, but in church, even I knew pretending was inappropriate. Being myself with others was uncomfortable, so I didn't socialize in church with kids my age. As a result, I had no friends my age in church then, so I just found a seat on the aisle in case I needed to slink off to hide in the bathroom.

They had turned the lights down, I figured to keep us quiet and create a dramatic moment, and I dutifully listened to every word. I heard about sin, a virgin birth, a cross, lots of blood, and a resurrection. It made sense and didn't make sense at the same time—if that makes sense. I wasn't sure really what to make of the story, but I could sense a stirring in me. I wanted to know more. Then the youth pastor said something that will stay with me the rest of my life. He said, "If you feel dirty, only Jesus can make you clean...and He wants to do that for you right now."

It was as if the earth was falling away beneath me, and all of a sudden a different way of living was being presented before me. I blinked and strained to hear what he said about becoming clean and I wondered how he knew. I didn't understand the crucifixion completely yet, but I knew sin and shame. I knew dirty and clean. I knew them better than this youth pastor could even imagine. So I was drawn to know more, to know how to be cleaned by Jesus. I sensed a hope rising within me that there was another way to live, for something other than what I had been carrying inside for so long. So I walked to the altar to talk to the youth pastor.

Well, no, I ran like a girl on fire.

I cannot count the number of times Jesus has continued to dive into my story. Of course, Jesus is with me always. His Spirit is living in me and has been resident in me from the moment I trusted in Jesus for my salvation. But especially in the beginning of our relationship, I was able to live for large chunks of time seemingly independent from Him. I had no need for Him to re-dive in to save me. That was finished. But what I didn't recognize immediately was how I needed Him in all my mini-messes, my tiny everyday dramas. Moving from being your own god to living with God is not unlike the adjustment to marriage after many years of singleness. The transition to living a yielded life takes time, intention, continual adjustments and a release of the demand to have life on your terms. While the blessings outweigh the sacrifices we make in our relationship with Jesus, dependency on His power and presence is a learning process. We exchange our dependency on our abilities and knowledge for a trust that Jesus has insight and capacity far beyond what we can understand. Yet even this exchange, this yielding, this choosing to trust Jesus in our little stories every day, is something we need His help to do.

With the help of Jesus over many years, I have practiced living in dependency on Him. Now I find myself depending on His presence with me frequently without giving it much thought, especially in this season of parenting a toddler. We joke about it, but I'm quite serious when I share how I am teaching my daughter the Gospel in 3 words: "Help me, Jesus." The longer version is: "Help me Jesus, I've got nothing." She knows both the shorter and longer versions because she hears them come out of my mouth daily, and she now uses them in her own undone moments.

I have collected many dive stories, times when Jesus rescued me while I was hurtling down a river of rocks battering against my soul. Times when I was wedged stuck, flailing to grasp a shore just beyond my reach crying out helpless seeking His help. We all have these stories, which is one of the reasons I wrote this book in the first place! A redemptive story starts with us in the place of stuck, needy, broken, giving up a helpless cry. This is the formation of our story, the beginning, the prognosis, the disease, the growing desperation and the reason Jesus came.

But the next plot point in every redemptive story is the Dive.

When I was 13 I learned that my father left us. I also learned that infidelity was involved. We instantly became a family of three and were left figuring out how to manage a family business that bore his name and where he played the essential role. We were devastated, naturally, and the trauma struck each of us a different kind of blow. For me, the abandonment was acute and the message received was that I was too much. And yet, I was also not enough. If I had been less heavy, ugly, dumb, foolish, demanding, needy, costly, he may have stayed with us. Or had I been more beautiful, smart, funny, gifted, spiritually wise, cheerful, light-hearted, he may have chosen us. The loss of a parent is never simple for a child, biological or otherwise. Abandonment fears root so deep, they can pop up for a lifetime even with God's faithful love steadily chiseling them down.

It was in that very season though, when God the Father entered my story in a bigger role than I Had given Him before. In a very real sense, God became my Father. I watched as He moved in mysterious ways to bring us through selling the house and business. He provided a safe place for us to live during a brief time of being without a home of our own. He provided unexpected cash in our mailbox, good employment for my mom as well as promotions so we could not only pay our bills, but we had enough so my brother and I could participate in school activities. He healed our bodies and kept us free from disease when we had no insurance.

He gave me enough focus, and good friends, to help me excel in school, and then used His connections to open a door for me to attend my dream university. He cared about my relationships too and listened to my cries at night. He was protective of my heart and nudged me out of relationships with guys who were "Mr. Right Now". I also experienced my Father carry me through heartache and bring me to a place of acceptance and forgiveness toward my earthly father, something I knew I could not do on my own.

It was October 8, 1998, I was a senior at the University of Notre Dame. It was in the wee hours of the morning—I had just hung up the phone after calling off an engagement. The now ex-fiancé was states away in graduate school; the call ended a five-year relationship. I took the ring off and put it in a drawer and cried myself to sleep for a few hours before I had to go to class. All I knew at the time was that God had been nudging me for weeks to end the relationship. It wasn't His path for my life and God was doing all He could to get my attention. I didn't know how I was going to get through the entire day without a ring on my left hand—I had worn it for 6 months and was used to it; and used to daydreaming happily about what it promised in my future. It felt like the longest day filled with the longest classes, and I had to pull over several times to cry secretly in bathroom stalls. But two things happened that day that changed the course of my history. In these two encounters, just as He did when I was 13 and fatherless, I believe God met me flailing down a rocky river.

First, when I got back to my dorm later that day, after classes were all finished, I checked my mailbox. I wasn't expecting anything from anyone, so when I saw a small box I was intrigued. And even more so when I read that it was from my great aunt in Florida, who never wrote to me before nor has since! I stood with the mailbox door hanging wide open while I ripped the box open to see the contents. Inside was a small clear bag with a tissue and a little card. The note said that this was my Nana's ring, that it was over 100 years old, but that she would have wanted me to have it, and that it probably wouldn't fit but I could wear it on a necklace or something. And, she loved me. What you don't know, and what she probably forgot, was that I have big fingers except for my left hand. I have a birth defect on my left hand where my fingers grew together like a catcher's mitt. I've had over a dozen surgeries through my childhood to separate my fingers and have movement. I wasn't supposed to really be able to do anything with my fingers, but that isn't the case in light of the fact that I'm typing these words at 55 wpm. Of all my 10 fingers, the only finger my Nana's ring fit on was the one that wore an engagement ring just hours earlier. My great aunt wouldn't know of the break up for days, but God knew. My perfect Father knew I'd need a ring that day, on that finger, and with that ring I believe He promised me I could dream again of a good future with Him as my first love.

The second thing that happened that day was less moving, at least for me at the time. I was thanking God for the ring, crying, praising Him for being all-knowing and all-seeing and all-loving toward me, in spite of all my mess. Right about that time was when He reminded me of my dad, a man I had no intention of inviting to that wedding and hadn't spoken to in 8 years. I reminded God of all this when I sensed Him nudge me to pray for him and keep praying for him daily. Had God not just put a ring on my finger, literally, I may have ignored Him. But He had my fresh awe and attention. I agreed to pray for my dad, but I knew I'd have to leave post-it notes everywhere just to remember him. So I did. Even then, the only prayer I could wholeheartedly muster was, "God... Dad...get him." That slowly evolved to, "God...Dad...do what you will with him." They weren't the best prayers, but God didn't ask me for good theology, just that I would pray for him.

That was October of 1998, and in December of 1998, just two months later when I was home for Christmas break, the phone rang. It was my dad. My brother jumped on the other phone and for maybe only ten minutes we chit-chatted about who knows what. Somewhere in the blur of the conversation my brother and I agreed to meet him and his new wife (not the woman he left our family to be with), for supper one evening. But before I hung up the phone I had one question pressing against the receiver. I asked hesitantly, "Dad...why now? I haven't talked to you in 8 years. You have missed high school and college. Why are you calling us now?" There was silence. Then he spoke, and his voice cracked, "Honey, I don't know how to explain it, but for the past couple of months it is like something has had me by the throat and I cannot shake it, so I had to reach out."

God...Dad...get him.

My Father had my father by the throat and was making a way for me to grow in my healing journey, against all odds.

My Father dove into the river of humanity's filth, and into my rocky river, for me.

And He does it for all of us because we are the treasure He seeks.

DISCUSSION QUESTIONS
7—THE DIVE

YOUR REDEMPTION STORY

What was your life like right before you responded in faith to Jesus?

_____

_____

Describe the moment you heard the Gospel and put your trust in Christ to forgive your sin.

_____

_____

_____

OTHER REDEMPTIVE STORIES

Recall a time when you found yourself "hurtling down a rocky river". Maybe it was a break-up, or a financial hardship, a loss, a decision that wasn't going as you planned. What were the circumstances? How did you feel? What were you tempted to believe?

_____

_____

_____

How did you experience Jesus come for you in that place? Was it what you prayed for, or did it come in a way that surprised you? Was a passage or story in Scripture meaningful to you? Did God use other people to meet you there?

_____

_____

_____

8

the Opening

"And there is no creature hidden from His sight,
but all things are naked and open to the eyes of Him
to whom we must give account."
—HEBREWS 4:13

I heard the diver. I heard him say he came down for me, to rescue me from all my mess. I knew I couldn't rescue myself, I had tried to cope, to manage, to make the best of the wreck growing inside of me. I wasn't sure I could trust him, I didn't know what was next, where he'd take me, or whether things would get better for me. He said he could remove all my burdens, it seemed too good to be true! He said he would need to open me, and though it terrified me to think of being seen like that, to be known and to have him see my ugly wound I was trying desperately to cover, I was done trying to do this life in my own strength. At the same time, I marveled at the thought of being opened, finally giving up all the pretending, the striving to keep it all together. I was clamped so tight, tangled up inside, I figured if he could open me, if he could get out of me what I couldn't get out, he could have me. I believed this diver. I believed he knew what I didn't. So I simply did what an oyster can do, which isn't much. I believed he came for me, that he had what I needed, even though I wasn't sure what that was myself. It wasn't a moment with fireworks, nothing spectacular really, I just trusted the diver was the one who could help me.

And would you know that simply trusting in the diver was all it took! In that instant we were surfaced above the deep, I was out in the air light and free, opened up before the kindest face. I'll never forget the kindness either. That was when I knew I was loved, when I knew I was finally safe. Why else would someone go to the sacrifice and trouble of going to the dark deep where terrible things happen, except for love? His hands held me gently, caring for my weak frame. As he touched my tender wound I felt a pressure, slight and steady. He was inspecting me, I never imagined ever allowing this before, but he assured me he knew what he was doing. With him was the farmer, that's what the other rescued oysters called him. Oh yeah, there were others. Many were opened and praising the diver, thanking the farmer. There were a few though who were still closed. They had heard the diver, they heard him with me even. They had been given the same opportunity to trust him too, but never opened. I don't understand why, maybe they'd open later. The farmer spoke with the diver as he gently worked around in my shell, I seemed to be crying out the pain as they carefully snipped and cut, but it was a different pain from the wound itself. It was like a healing release kind of pain. They hadn't pried me apart recklessly, I wasn't "shucked" as I had heard happens to some. They moved carefully, with precision and swiftness, with sterile tools that shone with cleanness. It hurt and time seemed to stop, but the clock said it all happened at once. Before I knew it the strain of carrying that burden within me was over. They had removed my immovable wound, and when it was finished I felt light as a spat again. I was going to live, and live freer than I had ever imagined!

I'm sitting in a coffee shop as I write this, it's Christmas time and gift-giving is in full swing. But I'm struck by the deeper paradoxical truth contained in a simple sign mounted over a tower of mugs:

"GREAT GIFTS AT GREAT PRICES"

The defining characteristic of a gift is that it costs nothing to receive. There is no price to pay as the recipient of a gift. If a recipient has to pay something, it is not a gift, it's a purchase using earnings. A true gift is simply that, a gift. No strings, no conditions, no purchase of any amount involved, and only then can it be received as a gift. Purchases are not gifts, not even deeply discounted purchases. They just can never be the same things. However, the gift first cost someone something to give it. The gift first had to be obtained by the giver, maybe even at a great price. Or, the giver had to willingly give up the value of owning the thing in order to give it to the recipient. Either way, a loss has to be incurred in a gift exchange, but to be a gift the loss has to be incurred by the giver, in some way. Accordingly, the only appropriate response for the recipient of a gift is always only gratitude.

Receiving gifts is awkward for many of us because we are trained to purchase everything. We buy shelter, food, coverings, even a sense of love in so many ways. Receiving gifts is vulnerable, it is a mystery, but it is as if we are being opened up and seen and loved just as we are, with no earnings or repayment through performance. And being opened up, seen, exposed, looked at intently, can be terrifying when we have shameful places we are trying to keep hidden.

"He sent from above, He took me; He drew me out of many waters. He delivered me from my strong enemy, from those who hated me, for they were too strong for me. They confronted me in the day of my calamity, but the LORD was my support.

He also brought me out into a broad place;

He delivered me because He delighted in me."

—PSALM 18:16-19

I know a woman who shared once that she "gave her heart to Jesus" one time, but it didn't work, nothing happened. She described no special feeling or sensation in the moment she says she prayed, and so it "didn't work for her." This breaks my heart because the sensation is not the salvation. We can trust new spiritual life is born within us based on sensation about as well as we can trust conception of life within us by sensation. We just cannot. While some people do experience a dramatic emotional, even physical response, to being freed from sin's claim on their souls through trust in Christ, it is not an indicator of whether or not our salvation is complete! If this was the case, we wouldn't need faith at all! But faith is the key over and over. It is simple, child-like, nothing fancy and yet life-altering faith that pleases God.

And while the sincerity of the faith is important, it doesn't have to be without questions. The faith can be thread bare, moth-eaten, holy even with holes, because it is what the faith is in that makes the difference. A rich, deep, sure faith in a two-legged chair is faith poorly placed. The only thing sure about the outcome is that a topple is coming. At the same time, we can be hesitant and hoping, and simply choose to sit down on a solidly built 4-legged chair believing it will hold us up, and find we never budge. Our security in the seat is not because our faith is sturdy, but because the thing we put our faith in is rock solid.

Thankfully we aren't being asked to put our faith in a two-legged chair, or even a 4-legged chair. We put our faith in the One who made all chairs, who made gravity, who made the ground we topple upon, and who lovingly picks us back up every time.

Jesus arrived on the scene as a human several thousand years *after* He partnered with God and the Holy Spirit to create the dusty earth that would later absorb His blood. When Mary was approached by the angel Gabriel, she knew the prophecies about the Messiah. She understood He would come in the line of David, that He would be the King of the Jews and He would usher in a

Kingdom that would reign forever. What shocked her was that He was coming, in her belly!

The promised Messiah was the hope for Israel. There were hints of hope for Gentiles from the beginning of creation, but the Jews knew the importance of the Messiah's coming better than anyone. Hope of salvation for the Gentiles is the mystery of the Gospel revealed in the pages of the New Testament. Tucked into the fabric of God's redemption plan with Jesus' cross and resurrection we find healing of the curse placed on Adam and Eve, redemption for Jews and a glorious opening for all non-Jewish men and women to come into the family of God by faith in Jesus the Messiah. God's family would be in number like the sands on the seashore, just as He told Abraham it would.

Had there been no cut, no wounding irritation, there would have been no redemption by Christ.

And there would have been no pearl, a Church formed and retrieved by God's infinite grace.

Salvation has nothing to do with what a recipient pays. If it does, it isn't a gift. We are recipients of grace, insufficient saviors, hopeful sit-downers. We have as much claim to our redemption and restoration as an oyster has to being freed of her burden.

God removes from us the burden of sin and shame we could not remove on our own. He gives us hearts of flesh, a regenerated spirit alive to respond with new appetites, new desires, new affections and abilities.[40] This removal and regenerating work is of God's Spirit, not of our doing. It is impossible for us to open ourselves, to "give" ourselves to Christ, to save ourselves, to forgive ourselves, to rescue ourselves from the prison of sin.

It is Christ who dives down for us, who retrieves us, who opens us up to a saving trust in His life for ours. Our part is found in believing. We receive the gift. This is it. And this is everything.

This is the Gospel:
Jesus lived perfectly.
Jesus died for our sins and was buried.
Jesus rose again.[41]

MY REDEMPTION STORY

I heard the diver. I heard Jesus telling me He had come for me, that He could make me clean. I didn't understand everything the youth pastor talked about, but I knew dirty, I knew clean, I knew possible and impossible. With me, clean was impossible, but I heard Jesus say it was possible with Him, but Him only. It seemed too good to be true, that He could love me. But why would He come to this dusty earth where we kill each other, just to be killed Himself, except for love? I was clamped so tight, the sin and shame were so tangled, my faith in a Savior felt slippery and thin but I was done trying to figure myself and my life out on my own. If God could help me, even if we had to get it all out on the table, I was ready. I wasn't sure He could open me up, if I could be cleaned, if the chair would hold me, but I was tired of standing on my own feet and plopped down on the cross of Christ for my sin. I believed Jesus that night. I believed He came for me, and that He had what I needed...that He was *who* I needed.

In that instant of belief, I was saved. My spirit was breathed into by the life of God's Spirit, born new to live forever with Him. I know this because of what God's Word says about salvation, it comes by faith in Jesus, and that is what I had. That simple faith swelled into an effervescent joy but nothing radical to speak of, no fireworks. The pastor finished the talk with an invitation for anyone who chose to trust Jesus to clean him or her, to come and pray together. The only prayer I had ever uttered knowingly was the one before I went to sleep, but I was compelled by the love Jesus had for me to go and pray. I went to the front and bent down on the altar steps. I remember gray and blue nubby carpet and for a split second I realized being forgiven meant Jesus saw everything that was in me. *All* the wild. *All* the dirty. But just as quickly came the realization of His love. Grace washed over me and my newly opened soul seemed to widen letting out everything I was afraid of anyone knowing. My DNA is probably still identifiable in that carpet I soaked in tears. But with those tears came such relief, like I dropped a lead weight with each one shed. Along with my confession went all the pressure inside of me built up from years of trying to be clean on my own, worthy of acceptance and love.

Jesus not only cleansed me from a permanent stain of sin, but he removed from me the burden of shame I had been carrying in my attempts to cover my sin. I was freed, finally, light and free. Shame wouldn't be finished with me, but my soul could be finished with shame because of Jesus' death and resurrection.

I left that night a new person, a baby, but brand new. The old Heather would never return to my home. My heart, my mind and my eyes were open. I once was blind, but now I could see.

"But you are a chosen generation, a royal priesthood, a holy nation, His own special people, that you may proclaim the praises of Him who called you out of darkness into His marvelous light; who once were not a people but are now the people of God, who had not obtained mercy but now have obtained mercy."[42]

This was Israel's story, but from this moment on, it was now my redemptive story too.

God has opened many doors in my life, doors I never could have opened on my own. I believe it was God who made it possible for me to attend the University of Notre Dame, and who later opened the door and held my hand through law school at the University of Florida. I mean, I was a good student and hard worker, and I love to learn. But God and I knew what I really brought to the table, and it wasn't enough to explain the opportunities I was given! My gifting was wrapped up more in my sheer belief that God wanted to do something through me, than in me being gifted in what I was actually doing. I believed God was with me in every class, job, internship, organization and service project, working in some purposeful way to do something meaningful even if it was a word spoken at the right time. It wasn't easy though. I was constantly aware of my gaps in every space I filled, afraid others would find out I didn't really know what I was doing. I'd have moments of lucidity, like I would understand really well what my role was and how I could make the world better through my work, but this was rare. Most of the time the magic was in the connections I made with the people I was working alongside, the conversations shared over a meal or while engaging with others on a project. It was easy for me to go deep with others gently but quickly, effortlessly really. Before we knew it, regardless of the titles we held, we were enjoying real life together.

But in law school the fear of being caught as a "fraud" reached a high pitch I couldn't ignore. It was my first semester my first year, I was a "1L" taking all the first-year law student courses like Torts, Contracts, Criminal Law, Ethics, Property and Legal Research & Writing. I had just finished working in publishing, doors God opened for me after college. While my job afforded me some amazing opportunities to travel the world, I was also in the middle of some hard talks with God about being single. I also began grieving adolescent wounds that were thawing after the deep freeze of years of emotional numbing. It was one of the hardest seasons of my life emotionally and spiritually, but I felt I had no time to process it all because I had a million pages to read each day for school.

Most law schools are known for employing the Socratic method for learning, which means you undergo a debate with the professor on a subject. Scrutiny and questioning are designed to draw out understandings, definitions, and my biggest fear: gaps.

A fraud's worst nightmare is close inspection. Administration never denied that one of the goals was to belittle you into an inch-high person, and it was often a goal reached. I had been in school for six weeks and had avoided being called on so far, but as each day passed my anxiety mounted higher because I knew my day was coming! I unconsciously hatched my plan, and it was to read everything, every case, every problem, and know it all. The problem was, I didn't know what I was doing, and no matter how hard I tried, I couldn't understand everything I read. The other problem was that my eyes would close each day, like clockwork. It was like I was built to sleep on a daily basis. But no matter how much I limited my sleep, and I really limited it—as well as eating and talking to people and doing absolutely anything else other than study—the hours in a day didn't add up to cover the amount of work assigned. Every day around 4:30pm I'd go home after class and cry hard for 15 minutes, just to release the pressure from the anxiety, fear and unresolved grief piling up inside. I lived with my closest friend, Sara, who graduated from college with me. Of all places, she was accepted into a PhD program at the University of Florida. For so many reasons God kept Sara close to me. She knew some of what I had been through and what I was processing. Each day that first semester in law school Sara would come home from her own classes and ask me if I cried again that day. Each day I would say yes, and she would give me a hug and then would cook supper and invite me to eat something. She had no idea how God was healing me through her friendship.

But one night when she came home, she found me still crying. She cooked supper and I couldn't eat, because I couldn't stop crying. I was hitting bottom, and all Sara could do was pray for me. I had come to a place where my need was beyond my ability to meet it any longer. I needed rescue. I was so depleted I could hardly make out my requests to God sensibly. I knew I was saved, I knew God's Spirit was within me, I knew I was eternally safe from being separated from God because my faith in Christ sealed my soul.

Chicken marinated in seasoned oil can never become unseasoned again, so I was comforted in the truth that who I was could not be undone, and yet I felt undone. My soul felt like it was passing emotional kidney stones, and I couldn't stand up straight from the pain. I remember uttering this to the Lord in that place, "God, no one wants what I have with You, not this, not this anxiety and stress and fear. I'm no witness of Your goodness now, I'm miserable and terrified and so angry I don't know what to do. I can't stand the pressure, it's too much. I told You I wasn't smart when I applied, You know me! You know what I bring to the table, Abba! I thought You had a plan though and now I'm here exposed and I'm going to be ridiculous. Are You going to be honored when I'm made to look like an idiot? It's coming! And by the way, if *this* is as good as life with You gets in this life, if this is as close as I can get to You, then I'm ready to come Home. I want more than this, I want more of You, more peace, more of Your life in my life, I'm desperate."

In this moment I remembered a class at church a friend had asked me to attend with her. I croaked at the thought. It was the last thing I wanted to do that night, go hear more about how to be a "good Christian" and force smiles, handshakes and endure empty clichés about hope. I told God no. I had great excuses, no one would even blink at them. But God continued to nudge me about it, so I yielded. I was afraid to get behind the wheel with all the crying that continued, and I told God how He was going to have to drive me there and back safely if He wasn't planning to bring me Home that night.

I didn't know what I would do to distract my friend from my tear-stained face, but being late helped. I slunk into a chair and gave a quick wave to affirm I was checking the box by showing up, and then retreated back into my shell with God. The video started for the study, and as the man on the tiny screen spoke I heard the diver. I heard Jesus telling my soul again how He had come for me, to this dusty earth, to my neighborhood, to my season in law school, for me. He reminded me how I was saved by faith alone in Him. He reminded me what I did to be saved, that it was my simple belief in His ability to cleanse me and restore me to God, and how it had nothing to do with what I could offer Him or anyone. That night God taught me about grace, the favor of God, the opening of doors when I deserved none of it. I knew mercy and forgiveness, I knew about His cross of suffering for my sin. What I did not yet understand in practice was the resurrection, the grace, the unmerited goodness of God that blessed me with gifts to share with others and a path that He marked out uniquely for me. The tears dried up within me as I instead felt a surge of hope returning, a flow of life refueling my soul. I didn't know exactly what this "grace" would mean for me in "law" school, but I knew God's timing was more than ironic. When I returned home I was exhausted and just wanted to sleep for days, but out of habit I cracked open one of my ten-pound books. I tried to read but the words just seemed to play hide and seek, and I sensed a nudge in my soul to rest, that God would direct me with studying later. I was too tired to argue and was refreshed with hope that God really did want to walk with me through this season, so I drifted off to sleep.

Over the next couple weeks, I practiced paying attention to that gentle nudge in my soul. It was a new rhythm of listening to my inner self, the real me in communion with God. I desired His Word more too, and began reading Scripture first in the morning, instead of torts. I asked God to show me how to study, what to study, how to be the best student I could be, you know, as myself. I still disciplined myself to sit and open my books. I didn't expect God to just download information into my mind while I watched hours of whatever was on television at that time. But I'd talk to God in my soul as I read for an assignment, and if the words started to dance around and make no sense, I'd simply move on. I'd open another book, start another assignment, and kept going until I understood something. If someone would come up to me and ask me a question, I'd answer it but I'd give them my whole self, listening again to what God might be saying in me and through me. Sometimes these exchanges would be quick and simple, but sometimes they'd become something rich and beautiful, and my reading assignment wouldn't get finished. I trusted all of this to God and though it felt risky, I yielded to an unseen plan God had for me, to His grace for me in law school.

Then a Tuesday came. The Monday night was one of those richer and beautiful connection stories, so the assignment for torts didn't get finished, and now it was Tuesday, tort day. I only had 15 minutes before class started when I had a flash of panic. I heard some other students discussing cases from our assignment and I had no recollection of the words at all. For a moment I questioned everything I was doing. I sat down and quickly opened my book, flipping through the cases trying to grasp understanding of everything on a high level, but it was futile. I closed my book, and my eyes, and said a quiet prayer under my breath asking that God would simply be with me, be seen through me and do whatever He wished with me. When I opened the book back up it was more out of curiosity than clamor, and I settled on a problem set, problem #4 to be exact. It seemed like a waste of time, we had never covered the problem sets and we were half way through the semester. But as I read, I understood what I was reading, and found it interesting. One thing I had learned in my new listening practice was to slow down and pay attention to what I found interesting, so I meditated on that little problem for the remainder of my time, then gathered my things and went into class.

Now, my torts professor was your classic "drill sergeant" law professor you see in the movies, with an alphabet full of credentials at the end of his name. He is retired now, but in my day even the soldiers in our class would stall outside the room, dreading the next hour. Professor Pearson was brilliant, socially distant with students, unimpressed, intolerant of excuses and committed to his standards with no apologies or exceptions. He was most famous for calling on a student who would be "on" for the day, inevitably releasing the class to a collective sigh of relief as the "hot student" was responsible for leading the class in the lesson through a grueling tête-à-tête with the professor. Oh, and the books had to stay closed. If the student was unable to do it for any reason, he'd tell that student to leave. His or her grade would instantly drop by a + or − increment, and everyone in the class would throw up a little in their mouths while he scrolled the roster for the next victim. And unfortunately, this was more common than not, so showing up to class without knowing the cases was madness! I debated skipping, but I learned too much during the class to let one pass me by, so I walked in simply believing that even if I was made a fool in class that day, that somehow God would use it for His purposes.

My name wasn't called though. He called on another student and I thanked God for sparing me another day. I took out my notes and right as I was about to date the page I heard Professor Pearson ask the student to take us through the problem sets. The room went silent, no paper ruffled, no pens glided, there was complete silence. This was a first for us, and in that moment you could tell it caught the student off guard too. Big time. The professor didn't skip a beat though, and as he opened his book (which again we were not allowed to open), he asked specifically for problem #4.

You read that right.

It was my problem. And soon, it would be *my* problem.

After that student left the class, he called on another, but then they left. And another, then they left. It seemed to go on for days, one student after another having to leave the room unprepared to go over problem #4. The professor paused to give a speech on the integrity of our generation, of our inability to do what we are asked, to rise to the challenges of our day. I didn't hear all of it for the sound of crying and murmuring by a guy sitting behind me, I was pretty sure. At the end though, with his back to the class as he wrote the next day's assignment on the board, he called my name. He also said I was allowed to leave without responding since I was likely not prepared, but instead I spoke up as loud as my quivering voice could project and gave the legal reasoning behind problem #4.

This time the professor gave another speech, and my eyes were trembling so bad from holding tears back, I only caught snippets of what he said. I heard something about integrity and how some people will do great things or something. After class I was swarmed with students wanting to know how I managed to make time to study everything, and how I understood what was going on in class. Still weak from adrenaline draining through my legs, I was mystified myself over what had just taken place, but I knew this was a holy moment. I told the students how I couldn't give them any major tips because I simply prayed that God would help me study. From that day on some called me the girl who "studies with God". I figured that about summed me up. Whenever the fear of being a "fraud" tries to bully me, and it still does, I remember that day in tort class. I remember how God opened my soul to experience His grace in a fresh way. I remember how I was spared in that tort class because of His faithful provision for me, not my massive intelligence. I remember how I was safe, in the deepest way, and that opening to God was opening to the One who would only give back to me in greater measure as I trusted my little to Him.

DISCUSSION QUESTIONS
8—THE OPENING

YOUR REDEMPTION STORY

Describe a time when you were forgiven for something and you doubted the person really forgave you. It seemed too good to be true. Did the person really show you forgiveness by moving on?

_____

_____

_____

How did it feel to receive God's forgiveness through Christ's sacrifice for your sin? Did you struggle believing God completely forgave you? Did you wonder if some of your sin stayed on you and didn't go on Christ's body on the cross? Do you sometimes wonder if He'll hold some sin against you still? (Spoiler alert: He won't.)

_____

_____

_____

OTHER REDEMPTIVE STORIES

Have you ever been afraid of being found out as a "fraud" in some way? Are you ever afraid people will see you still sin? Describe how you handle it when you do sin. (Because we ALL do friend!)

_____

_____

_____

What has grace meant in your life? How have you come to notice God's grace in your everyday life—in your relationships, your roles, your routines?

_____

_____

the Washing

"...Christ loved the church and gave Himself for her, that He
might sanctify and cleanse her with the washing of water by the
word, that He might present her to Himself a glorious church,
not having spot or wrinkle or any such thing, but that she
should be holy and without blemish."

—EPHESIANS 5:26-27

*I was loved; the diver gave everything just to have me here, in his hands.
Everything that needed to happen to make me his own had been done,
nothing left was needed and I could finally rest.*

*But I saw some other oysters going into a bath. I didn't understand
what it was about, what it was for, and why they needed it. I wondered
if maybe something was still wrong with me, if I needed to do something
more to be acceptable to the diver and the farmer. I still had remnants of
the boring sponge, the snail drills, the work of whelk actively chipping
away at my shell, bent on consuming me one slow bite at a time.*

*I heard the farmer's gentle reassuring voice, and I calmed down. He
spoke of washing, of sanctifying, and I realized he had more in mind
for me, but it was all for my well-being. He told me I was his, and just as*

he loved his own body, nourishes and cherishes it, so he would nourish and cherish me. If there was one thing I was learning, it was that oyster farmers know the best way to wash away the things that eat away at us.

Salt.

So he swirled me in the brine bath, and as I soaked in that high salinity, all my enemies fell away. All became quiet within me as I took in the wonder of what was happening. I had not only been rescued from a dark pit, I was not only saved from carrying an eternal burden, and I was not only welcomed into a loving companionship with my rescuer; but now he was setting me up to live a new and different kind of life. A cleaner life. Cleaner, not because I wouldn't have troubles again, but because the farmer had a salt bath and I could swirl in it regularly.

My daughter is my daughter, and nothing can change that fact. She became my daughter through adoption, and just as we are adopted by God and don't call Him our "adoptive Father" but simply call Him Father, so too I am simply Mommy, Mama, Mama Bear, Mom. Our relationship is secure, her identity is sealed in our family and I am bound to her as she is bound to us. This is the Gospel story, really, of a parent adopting a child, meeting the requirements to become her parent and then giving her a completely new identity. The old is gone, the new has come, never to be the old again. Intestacy laws recognize this dynamic, and an inheritance passes to children legalized or birthed because the new family born is the family that lives on forever. Even "open" adoptions, no matter the arrangement, do not change the fact that the "real parents" are the legally recognized parents who experienced the birth of their child through the labor pains of adoption.

This is a big deal to us, but it should be a big deal to all of us who sit under the Gospel for our identity and security. When who we are today is defined in terms of who we were before

Jesus met all the requirements for our adoption by God, we can waffle under doubt of our security as His children. God is always perfectly confident in His identity as our Father, but we can feel all sorts of insecurities as we continue to identify ourselves with our past self and not our new selves. In fact, this is right where the irritant likes to strike us, by telling us we are who we used to be, that nothing has really changed. He tells us we don't really belong in God's family, that we will never be truly accepted as His own beloved child. Most of our struggles in this life are not with the things we struggle to release or move into but are rooted in a misunderstanding of our identity. God's enemy casts a shadow of doubt over our identity, and in so doing casts a shadow of doubt over the Gospel. Who we are is just too big of a deal to not get it right.

It doesn't mean we ignore our past completely, or that it doesn't matter, or even that it cannot be received as lovely. Our formation is still part of us and helps to draw us into God's fuller story unfolding in our lives. When my daughter was just a baby, I would rock her in my arms and tell her where she came from, how she came to be mine, and who she came from before. Even though she was only able to take in milk, I needed the practice in making our conversation natural. I want to always tell her her story, and in that little rhythm I practiced getting use to the words rolling off my tongue into her ears. We continue to share appropriate pieces of information for her age and are committed to satisfying her curiosity as best as parents can reasonably and wisely satisfy their children's questions about life. We don't make this a priority because we care about adoption as a theological concept, though it is one. We share her formation story with her because we are parents, and this is what parents do: we help our children understand who they are, but in the context of God's big story. While we are telling her *her* formation story, it is with the goal of pointing her to *His* story. We will tell her also of our pursuit of her, our desire for and choosing of her, of a final hearing and a proclamation of a new name for her. We will affirm her belonging, her place with us that was decided long before she was even conceived. Her security as our daughter is sealed, no further proof is needed, it is finished. This is what the Gospel assures us of as God's children. It is in God's design of us, in His pursuit of us, and in His sacrifice for us that we form our full identity. But if we don't intentionally cling to the Gospel, to God's Word that tells us who we are, to the Adoption Decree that is sealed and locked away, then we will be vulnerable to deception that calls us by a former name causing us to doubt our belonging, eating away at us bite by bite.

Yet how unloving would it be if when my daughter was a baby, I clapped my hands and said, "Ok, now you're my daughter, it's all finished", but then I neglected her daily nutritional needs. What if I failed to bathe her or refused to create a safe environment for her. What if I withheld touch and comfort from her on a regularly basis, and never gave her the opportunities she needs to develop into a competent woman someday? I think you would agree it would be cruel. Yet so often we don't recognize God's ongoing work in our lives as His parental love and doting attention as our Father, strengthening and guiding us into our destinies. Shame filters His efforts to care for our needs and shape our character as His rejection of us. We mistakenly interpret His correction and stretching of us through challenges as His punishment of us for being imperfect.

Now in my 40s, I can say I've grown in my understanding that being a parent is not about biology as much as it is about nurturing. A few definitions of "mother" that especially draw my attention are, "to bring up (a child) with care and affection"[43] and, "to give rise to"[44]. The job of being a "mama" is not about birthing a baby as much as it is a commitment to live your life so you nourish and cherish other lives into fruitful adulthood. A mama is not finished when the child is born, or born into her family, but continues on as she nurtures a young one, addressing various needs alongside a father physically, relationally, emotionally, and even spiritually. I am a selfish being, but if even I can recognize my child's daily need for washing, feeding, tending, stretching, comforting, and yes, even challenges for her own well-being, how much more does God have these things in mind for us? I don't stop nurturing my child just because she is mine finally, not on your life. If anything, because she is mine, now is when I really pull out all my resources and give her everything I have and do all I can to invest in her. I go to costly lengths to equip her to become who God created her to be when He saw her in the beginning. Not in the beginning when she lay in a womb far from me, but in the beginning when He made the heavens and the earth and crafted a redemption plan that featured her as a character in His epic story.

We have been rescued, delivered, adopted and are cherished as daughters, now and forever. Our worth has been decided, we are the costliest treasures of God, and the infinite price has been paid, never to be paid again. But in Their endless love for us, our Father who delights in us, and Jesus who redeems and displays us, are together always at work with the Holy Spirit within us; preparing us for the uniquely beautiful destiny we were made for ever since the beginning of all the things.

"I have wiped out your transgressions like a thick cloud, And your sins like a heavy mist. Return to Me, for I have redeemed you."

—ISAIAH 44:22

We are washed once for eternal life; it is the cleansing blood of Jesus that wipes out our transgressions. His blood sacrifice was shed so we wouldn't have to spill ours. Even if we could shed blood to settle our debt with God, only the holiest of blood will do, and we carry the corrupt nature of Adam and Eve. Our sacrifices, like the ones Israel labored for centuries to present before God, are wholly insufficient.

The Gospel gives us good news: the washing we most need has already been provided in the blood of Christ. No other washing, no other blood, is appropriate to transform our old lives into new ones and so guarantee eternal life with Him.

But what about Baptism?

I will confess something first. I used to think John the Baptist, was, ahem, Baptist. I was young and the Bible is lot to take in. But John "the Baptist" was Jewish, the second cousin of Jesus, also Jewish in case that needs to be clarified too. John was ministering to Jews; this was all for Jews. Gentiles had no context for baptism, or sacrifices. It was dictated to Jews under Jewish laws handed down from Moses by God. Jews understood the need for washing; most Jews practiced ritualistic washing under the law in preparation for offering various sacrifices. Priests especially underwent ritualistic washing before entering the Temple because failure to do so would end up in death![45] But the ceremonial washing of Jewish people was a *preparation* for reconciliation with God through sacrifice, not a transformational cleansing unto salvation. It was mostly unheard of to announce a remission of sins in conjunction with a water cleansing ceremony, especially with no visible sacrifice offered to reconcile sinners with a holy God.

There is a record, though, of a sect of Jews who lived in the area where John lived and ministered, that practiced a water cleansing ritual in conjunction with a commitment of the heart to live obediently before God. The Qumran community was a desert people known for their ascetic lifestyle, and for giving us the Dead Sea scrolls. According to their practice, washings of every kind were done, many times in a day. In their worship, it was only possible to become pure before God if during a certain water cleansing ritual the member be, "made clean by the humble submission of his soul to all the precepts of God."[46] This heart "submission" then was essentially the sacrifice offered during the bodily "immersion" practice, and this may have been the context influencing John's ministry of water baptism with repentance for the remission of sins. There are differences between John's ministry and the Qumran community though. They lived separate from the world and its institutions, but John engaged the religious, political and social facets of his generation. Also, though they too looked for the coming of God's Kingdom on earth, John's baptism brought with it the announcement that Messiah was coming and that this submission of heart observed by immersion of body was the preparation for His coming. Whether John was a member of the Qumran community or not, God was preparing Jews and all the world for a new kind of cleansing, and a new sacrifice through John's ministry.

John's mission was to catch the attention of a busy people who had no doubt grown dull in their delayed hope of Messiah coming. The world had experienced the silence of God for 400 years, and from a desert wasteland close to the Dead Sea, a voice cried out preparing a sleeping people for God's grand entrance. John's wild demeanor and popular baptismal ministry slowed the hurried and was blessed with multitudes responding with belief and expectant hope. There was opposition as the Jewish leaders who held secure places of influence through the law system were not eager to lose that power. They were likened to a "brood of vipers" in Luke's account, and would strike out at the Messiah in time. But God's ordinance to John to baptize with water for the remission of sins, preparing a way for the Lord's ministry about to start, was clear and John faithfully obeyed.

Yet there is no way John could have fully understood the impact of his ministry, the point of baptism, the richness of the symbolism in this simple act. Just as there is no way Moses could have fully known the impact of obeying God's ordinance to build the Temple, to follow the pattern set out by God that points to all of the Kingdom revealed. There is no way he could have understood the rich significance of those specifications. There is no way Noah could have understood the necessity of the ark's dimensions, the far-reaching implications of having one door that God had to shut for them Himself, sealing them safely inside until they were carried through the wrath of God poured out on all the earth. God's ways are mysterious; we are small-minded and take in God's complex manifold grace in the simplest expressions.

God made it plain for us as John pointed directly at Jesus when he revealed who the Messiah really was, God the Son. And whether he understood it yet or not, John's water baptism pointed everyone to a coming death and resurrection of new life Jesus would soon experience for our sakes. Baptism is the recognition of a burial and a resurrection, dead with Jesus and raised with Him to new life.[47]

So today, as we are baptized, it is an act of obedience to God and an expression of our faith in Christ that we too died and rose with Him, proclaiming our identity as new and found only in Jesus. It is a significant moment in the life of a believer, and often is an anchor that serves to embolden us when storms come to challenge our faith, because they do come. We can remember who we are, that we died with Christ and the life we live, we live by faith in the Son of God who was raised up to new life and raised us up to new life with Him. Some experience deep emotional and even physical responses to being baptized, just as some experience this upon salvation, but again, sensation is not the indicator of a real inner dynamic taking place. As it is faith that saves us, it is faith that strengthens us for the road ahead as a believer in an unbelieving world.

But the regenerating washing that we need for the road ahead is not only anchored by our baptism, it is actively engaged by our regular washing in the Word of God. This Word of God was breathed into 44 men who have written pages that consistently communicate the full redemption story of God for humanity. These pages have survived centuries of attempts to be eradicated through fire, banishment, restrictions and rebuffs. Countless attacks have been made against the proclamation of the Gospel and the stories recorded for our benefit, and yet it remains intact and continues to regenerate new babies in the faith in every generation. And as we study, meditate on and ingest this Word of God in daily meals, it does the hidden digestive work of breaking down and eliminating deceit's power in our minds. The truth of God regenerates our thoughts, giving us new thoughts so we think like children of God and not the children of wrath, as we once were.

Our position as children of God is sealed with the faith we put in Christ as our Savior, but just as a child continues to be bathed, and then grows up learning how to bathe herself so as to enjoy the fullness of health and vitality, so we too return to wash again and again in the Word of God that renews our minds and cleanses our consciences of all the dust of this world's system. Our loving Redeemer loves us too much to leave us the way we are at conversion, but in fact now that we belong to Him, we receive all the care and attention and investment as children.

> *"...For no one ever hated his own flesh, but nourishes and cherishes it, just as the Lord does the church."*
>
> —EPHESIANS 5:29

MY REDEMPTION STORY

In an instant of belief, when I put my trust in Jesus to forgive my sins, I was saved. The old me died and all my past sin, my present sin, and my future sin washed away by the cleansing blood of Christ. Just as a baby is given life through blood in the womb, so too I was given life through Christ's blood. As a newborn is welcomed into the world covered by blood, so too I was welcomed and covered. It was the blood of Jesus that gave me life and washed me clean; it was not of my own doing. I was starting over as a baby by faith, a child, and was adopted by God as His own daughter. There was and is no need for any other spiritual washing, no other sacrifice, no other cross or work for me to do in order for me to have eternal life with Jesus. He did it all and it was finished.

Soon after, I heard about being baptized. What little I knew about it came from mere mentions of it quarterly in the church we attended. For 2 months I would revel in the joy and security of being saved and loved by my Father, but then I'd hear announcements about baptism and would struggle with doubts. Was I really saved, since I had not been baptized yet? It wasn't that I didn't want to understand about baptism, or didn't want to do it, but I had questions and fears with no one to help me. I was delaying, and with every third month of announcements, deeper fears would strike at my peace.

One of the reasons for my delay was that our church at the time used a nearby river. Being in deep water was reason enough for me to resist, but also, I had been on that river, and other rivers like it. I had seen the snakes. (The irony is not lost on me that it was fear of snakes keeping me from baptism.) Another reason though was that I was a kid, and I only saw grown adults being baptized. It seemed like something only grown-ups did and that I probably needed to wait. I also just lacked understanding. Even at a young age I didn't want to do something just to look religious.

I also didn't want to commit to something I didn't agree with or believe. No one at our church was teaching what baptism actually was, or why we did it, and even when I asked questions all I got was, "Well, Jesus did it". I wanted to obey Jesus, but I needed help and prayed for understanding and courage.

It was ten years after I put my trust in Jesus that I sensed a nudge to be baptized. I had prayed about it, and nursed shame over it for a decade. I was a junior in college and was growing leaps and bounds in my faith as I learned more about Christ's finished work on His cross, and how that worked into my everyday life. I also learned about baptism, how it was a public proclamation of my faith to others, demonstrating my belief that I too was buried with Christ, and raised to new life. I had been proclaiming God's work in my life ever since I was saved, but I had a desire now to proclaim it through baptism and follow in the steps of Jesus.

In 1998, on July 26, I was baptized in the church where I trusted in Christ. I was engaged and planning a wedding and was about to return to college for my senior year. We were to be married a couple weeks after graduation, and I had a burning desire to be baptized before I was married. It was also good timing for another reason. The church built a baptismal in-house so it was completely snake-free. I remember the day clearly, because I was brimming over with joy and hope and expectancy. I knew I was sealed and secure through my faith alone, but that even more fueled my enthusiasm and readiness to proclaim God's work in my soul before a congregation. I wanted them to know that it was all Jesus, not me, and that I was once dirty but was now cleaned forever. And in the quiet of the night before, I asked God to do something new in me through this baptism experience. I knew nothing could change my eternal security, or add to how much He loved me, but I wanted more of His reign in my heart and so simply asked for His blessing on me!

What I didn't expect with that baptism experience was that He would make more room for Himself in my heart by removing the fiancé out of it first. God's ways are mysterious indeed! I can trace the end of my first engagement to July 26, 1998, and have been thanking God for reigning more and more in my heart ever since. I lost nothing that was worth holding onto and gained more of what I cannot live without!

And that wasn't the end of my washings. Since that season I have learned that I regularly need washing. Just as we continue to cleanse our physical bodies regularly, I continue to wash my mind daily with God's Word. It is the salt that removes all the enemies of my soul trying to bore deceitfully into my thought life. Regular washing keeps my mind fresh and energized to live and move in the grace of God. Though the blood of Christ cleansed me from sin and shame, I can still feel the effects of it at work in the world where I live, attempting to bore into me from the outside since it cannot fully reside within me. I feel the tension of being new in old skin. I can easily forget I was born anew, but my baptism serves as an anchor to remind me I was buried and rose again with Christ by faith. And I return to the brine bath of the Bible. The salt of truth eats away at the lies. I feel fear fall away. I find love washing me over and over with assurance.

It all happened. It is all finished. I am clean.

In the middle of writing this chapter I had to stop for one very good reason:

This woman needed a bath!

I have been writing in every stolen moment I can get: during nap times, extra early in the morning, during special childcare-provided hours, at red lights. My usual pace of house work, rest, social connecting beyond my husband and daughter, and yes, at times even everyday bathing has paid the price of sacrifice so I can get words to paper. This is unsustainable, of course. I've made my family my main priority during my non-writing time, and quiet rest a close second. No one needs to read words that flow from a rushed and exhausted soul. But as women often do, I have at times neglected my body this season. This says something deeper to me, but more than what my neglect says to me, is what God's loving attention for my body reminds me of today.

If I had a person in my life that I treated the way I have treated my body at different times over these 40 years, it is highly likely that person would not be on speaking terms with me today. That person would even be justified in obtaining a restraining order against me. My words and actions over many occasions have violated the many reasonable boundaries my body maintains for her dignity. I have blamed by body for misdeeds she never committed. I have spoken ugly to her, calling her names and have pointed out and relentlessly reminded her of all her flaws. I have mocked her, making her the brunt of my jokes in public. I have neglected her needs, making others more important than her often. I have abused her with bites at her nails, I have stuffed her with excessive amounts of food only to then deprive her of nutrition for hours at a time. I have chided her attempts to move, pushing her mercilessly to move faster than she was ready for, lifting more weight than she could bear safely, and rarely let her settle for anything less than perfection. I have forced her against her will into situations that do not fit her at all, pinching and squeezing her painfully so she can seem like someone she is not. And as she has aged, I've caught myself telling her she is losing influence, beauty, value and is becoming less-than. And yet, all the while, here she is with me, offering to serve me and help me enjoy my life.

We feel shame and then we give shame. Shame has to go somewhere. Few people in our lives will accept this kind of shaming without standing up to us at some point. It feels safer then to pour our shame out on ourselves with assaulting words or objects, bringing damage to both our bodies and our souls. It doesn't occur to us that we can do something altogether different with our shame, something that can leave us free and open to receiving love.

In my early 20s, when I was being drawn to know Jesus more, I started to notice His attention was on my attitudes toward my body. Every verse I read or message I heard brought me back to what I believed about myself, and about my body in particular. My first memory of my body was associated with the words, "birth defect". I shared earlier how I have a birth defect on my left hand where all my fingers were conjoined like a catcher's mitt. After birth I was immediately whisked away for my first of many surgeries to "fix" my "defected" body. Fixing my defects became a way of life, really. My body didn't understand it at the time, but apparently I believed I had to fix everything about me, from weight and skin to intelligence and personality, because it was all defected. This is what shame does, it takes a defection and makes you the defection.

Shame partners with pride too. Pride comes in when you're down and crowns you the emperor of your body. You are falsely deemed all authority to decide for yourself what "fixed" looks like. You are deceptively granted full power to do anything and everything to achieve perfection. But then pride lies to you again, now with promises of satisfaction if you ever reach perfection. Weakened with hate for your body, loaded down with negative feelings based on mistruths you believe about your worth, you see a carrot dangled in front of you with a false promise of hope of a good life if you only change your body. Sound familiar? "You don't really have a good life Eve, but you could if you only act independently of God." Eve's story reminds us that even if you reach the dangling carrot of bodily perfection you are going for, which rarely happens, the pleasure and moment is fleeting at best.

After years of wrestling with Scriptures like, "I am fearfully and wonderfully made....", and "...your body is the temple of the Holy Spirit who is in you...", God brought me to a place of surrender and reconciliation with my body. I remember the day still. I stood in front of a floor length mirror in a room at the front of my home, a guest room. Looking back that was the most appropriate place for me to reconcile with my body; after all, I was a guest dwelling within her. I stood there and started at the top, with my hair, and confessed everything I had done to hurt my hair. I know, this seems overly dramatic and silly, and I thought so too, at first. But it only took seconds of confessing all I had done to injure this body before me in the mirror, before I felt the full weight of my words and thoughts. I was cut to the heart, this was not my body, this was God's precious gift to me made with His own hands, and I was devaluing her at every turn. Of great surprise to me, it wasn't shame that was breaking my heart though, it was God's kindness. It was grace. Grace was washing over me as I was finally able to see the gift standing before me. For the first time I received from God's hands this creation, this work of art by His own definition, as the gift it was to me. As I asked for forgiveness through choking tears, I felt delight fill my soul, and saw my body in a new way. An appreciation started to form in my mind for aspects of my body I never imagined appreciating, so I spoke affirmations out loud to reinforce these new observations. I should have chiseled them in concrete while I was at it. Embracing ourselves with the grace of God is unnatural. We are constantly challenged by shame to reject grace, reject our bodies, reject our souls, reject goodness, reject community, and it is the supernatural Spirit of God who draws us back to the mirror with Jesus holding our hand.

Jesus came to give life to the dead, and His plans are for our bodies as well. He spoke often about the body. He used the image of a body to help us understand His love for us and His plans for our growth and healing. He has plans in place to fully redeem our bodies and restore them to a perfection we can only imagine. He uses both our strengths and our weaknesses together to accomplish His plans for humanity, and He is pleased with what we offer to Him.

Defects and all.

DISCUSSION QUESTIONS
9—THE WASHING

YOUR REDEMPTION STORY

Have you chosen to experience baptism yet? If not, what is keeping you from it?

_____

_____

_____

If you have experienced baptism, what motivated you to do so? Share your experience!

_____

_____

_____

OTHER REDEMPTIVE STORIES

How has your baptism experience shaped and supported your faith journey? Was it an anchor for you in expressing your public identity as God's child?

_____

_____

_____

How have you experienced God's Word in your faith journey? Have you seen Scripture as a book of rules or as an invitation to a deeper relationship with God? Do you see the need to regularly wash your mind in the purity of God's Word? If not, what do you do with destructive thoughts? If you do see the value of meditating on God's Word, describe how it has helped you.

_____

_____

_____

your Retrieval story

{This is where the Gospel and your faith meet! Keep it simple, let the Gospel do the heavy lifting...}

I was here _____ when I heard the Gospel of Jesus Christ:

> "...that Christ died for our sins according to the Scriptures, and He was buried, and He rose again the third day according to the Scriptures."
>
> —1 CORINTHIANS 15:3-4

I responded by believing Jesus died for my sins. I put my trust in Jesus' death, burial and resurrection to forgive me of my sins.

> God's Word says that it is by God's grace, His undeserved favor toward me, that I am saved through this faith alone.
>
> —EPHESIANS 2:8

I know my salvation is not based on how I feel, but this is how I felt after knowing I was forgiven and forever reconciled with God.

_____

_____

_____

_____

_____

_____

the Display

10

the Setting

"Every experience God gives us, every person
He puts in our lives is the perfect preparation
for the future that only He can see."

—CORRIE TEN BOOM

I spent five years in the deep with that burden swelling within me. Five years wondering, waiting for something I hoped existed, but wasn't sure what "it" or "who" it was. What would it look like? How would I recognize it? If I was supposed to find it, how would I here in the dark, stuck and alone? In my darkest moments I doubted it even existed, a way out, a love meant for me, a life of goodness, hope and peace. Five years may not seem like long to you, but sit on the bottom of anywhere in silence and in pain for five minutes, you'll be searching for another way too.

But five years of suffering now seems like nothing compared to the peace of being fully known and loved, pursued, provided for and watched over. The bulge pressing in on me from the inside is now out, and while I thought I wanted it to be destroyed and forgotten, tossed off to the farthest sea away from me, it would seem the farmer and diver had other plans.

What I once kept hidden away and barricaded off, is now being gently handled by the farmer and diver together. I don't know what they are preparing, but I can see other burdens, like mine, seated in these glorious thrones of shimmering silvers and golds. Light itself seems to be dancing brilliant and dazzling all over the face of the burdens, as if set to music for the delight of the farmer and diver.

I hear them talking, they are happy, and it dawns on me that they have been the whole time. How could they be happy working with my burden? How could they find any good from it? I hear them call my burden a name, a pearl. The sound of it is lovely, a lovely name for something unlovely, in my opinion. Others did me wrong, and I did others wrong. What good could come of the whole mess? Pearl was the part of my name I liked, but I always figured "Wild" told the real story. I would say they didn't know what they were doing, my stubborn burden was the last thing that deserved such a soft name, but they were clearly better at rescue and restoration than me.

The pearl, as they called it, was the color mauve, kind of small compared to the other "pearls" I could see around, but that didn't bother me. I knew how enormous it felt when it was crushing the life in me. After you've come through something so life consuming, and experience rescue, no one can diminish the value of your pearl.

What I couldn't understand though was why they were delighting so much in it, in me, in this whole situation! It wasn't that they delighted in me being wounded, I could tell they hated my suffering in the way they gently cared for me. Their kindness persuaded me that they wanted my healing, not pain for pain's sake. But I watched how they cared for my pearl with such reverence, as if somehow the unholy had become holy. They assured me I would never carry that pearl again, ever. They said it was impossible to go back to what I once was, with that burden in me. I was enormously relieved but wondered what would come of my pearl. I couldn't help but soften toward her as I watched them care for her so intently.

They presented this fancy setting I never would have imagined being associated with me, but it actually fit her perfectly. Not too big, not too small. The metal shone so brightly, it flashed blinding bursts of white like reflections of sun on sea. Their hands were soft but swift, both moving together perfectly, using tools built just for their hands specifically designed to work with pearls. Before I knew it, they were fastening prongs around her, as if a hand with fingers closing around would hold her safely in a tiny shiny basket forever. The farmer's eye's watered and the diver's smile was as wide as the shoreline. They knew something I didn't, and it pleased them. They turned to show me their work, and I finally saw what they saw. She was altogether lovely, transformed from the tangled mess of sorrow within me into a glorious display delighting my hero's hearts. Had they simply discarded her, it would have been like it never happened, and the pain didn't matter. Now though, I felt understood, dignified, like they knew and appreciated the hardship she represented for me.

They had written their names on her surface, they were claiming her and me as their own, as treasures even. The plan was to send her out, so others could cherish her and hear our story and the tale of how the diver and farmer rescued me. People would marvel and want to know the diver and farmer who could fashion something lovely from my unlovely.

I was overwhelmed. It all seemed too good to be true. But it was true.

Our setting is not merely our social strata, economic status, our geographical location, our physical capability, our many genetic and logistical limits, intelligence, gifts or talents. Our setting is the generation in which we have been born, the season of humanity we live in, the space on the timeline of God's story unfolding. We may have power to influence many aspects of our setting, but our place in history is a non-changing reality. For such a time as this we are here on this earth by God's design. As such, both the privileges and traumas of our age are an essential part of our story and work to shape us according to God's ultimate plan so He can use us according to His ultimate purpose.

Neither of my parents were encouraged to pursue an education beyond high school, though both are incredibly bright and talented. They had spunk though and sought employment where they could learn and grow in expertise. While the thought of becoming professionals, business owners, elected officials or millionaires may have been furthest from their minds, God was steadily directing them into opportunities that brought out their natural strengths. After my mom trusted in Christ, she took my brother and I to church faithfully. Later, she and my dad started and grew a booming business with a good name known throughout all of northwest Florida. Integrity, excellence and speed were hallmarks of their business largely because of my dad's talent and my mom's faithfulness to God's principles of stewardship. Even after my parents divorced, my mom joined on with a major airline and climbed the management ranks over her successful career of 25 years.

In spite of the hardships of their marriage and the wounds of their past, God used my parents in their community and used their stories to make Him famous. Over the years my dad has shared with countless men trapped in destructive lifestyles about his own broken choices that caused wreck in his body, within his family and that shut down his once-booming business. His story is one of warning and caution, to slow down, to look up and get down on your knees. My mom has come alongside many women who struggle with shame, sorrow, who feel forgotten, overlooked, rejected and abandoned. She has taught women what Scripture says about renewing our minds in God's Word and encourages them to trust God's faithfulness no matter how dark their lives may get in some seasons.

For both of them, what could seem like failures in their stories God has put on display like pearls within the setting of timely relationships throughout their lives. He hasn't done it to embarrass them or bring them shame, hardly! He has derived great delight in watching them share their stories, giving them the privileged seat of watching other beloved humans discover grace, love, and kindness coming from the Father who loves and pursues them.

Even now I look over my own life from the vantage point of just turning 40 and I can already see God's mysterious working in the nature of my own rescue, my pearls, and the divine settings that I can see now fit me perfectly.

My growing up was split-level, with the first half of my adolescence under a roof with married parents, and the second half with a single mom and no father in sight. We didn't attend or watch college football games, we had no one to cheer for and my parents had no interest in sports. I'd see kids wear team colors during football season, telling stories of where their parents "went", but it made no sense to me. Higher education and professional careers were just not what we talked about at home. I never told anyone, but I thought the "colors" the kids wore were for special places their parents went to work after high school, and that they were just really passionate about their competitive jobs. As I entered high school though, I realized college was a thing, and it was where you went after high school, and was a really big deal.

Ever since I can remember, I've believed I was living inside an epic tale. I didn't think the story revolved around me, but I felt like an essential character. I wanted to be a wife and mother when I grew up, but in all my daydreams with my dolls there would be some major obstacle that would try to keep us apart. I'd imagine being swept off my feet by a warrior prince who couldn't resist me, who battled fiercely against all the foes just so we could be together, and that I would have to stand ground against arrows for us too. Of course, then I would "drive my kids" around to all kinds of activities, grocery shop, and we'd vacation as a big family at the beach.

As a pre-teen, I also wanted to be an astronaut, or a hairdresser. I had no real idea how either of these careers worked, but I loved brushing and styling hair for my dolls and younger brother, and the movie "Space Camp" won all my attention. In high school though I decided I would be a doctor because I wanted to help people and it seemed like the most direct and respectable way to do it. I was also desperate to impress my then-boyfriend's family which was filled with doctors. I saw myself as a poor and ridiculous girl, too much and yet not enough for them. I overheard one of the family members once describe where I lived as, "that neighborhood on the wrong side of town..." Wrong. Shame continued to show up in unexpected ways, and for a time I thought if I became a doctor maybe I'd finally be *right*.

My freshman year of high school was shadowed over by my father leaving, my parents divorcing, my mom selling everything and us moving in with my grandparents. My faith was in infant stages when trauma hit our family. It would seem this life with Jesus would not come easy. My soul did the best it knew how, with such little awareness of how to meet my needs and my parents in such pain. What I couldn't calm with eating, I'd cover in performance. This was the beginning of my quest to get into the best university with the highest standards. I didn't know how I'd actually get in, but I was determined to go, but not just to prove myself. I also had that deep abiding sense of destiny, and a desire to become who God said I was even though I didn't know what that meant. Like my parents, I was often overwhelmed by grief and pain, because even though Jesus had saved me and brought me into new life by faith, I still had a lot of hurt places that needed His on-going restoration. My mind was yet tangled up in a lot of areas and washing my thoughts with His truth was a slow, daily, long-distance race, and I was addicted to sprints.

But the presence of Christ in me nudged me ever closer to who I really am, reminding me that I was created for a purpose in my generation. I loved being on the stage performing in concerts and musicals, but shame was telling me to hide away, that I had no business being known and seen and enjoyed. I heard that I had nothing to offer. Yet God's Spirit kept whispering hope of something grander than I had imagined for myself, something that fit me uniquely. My wounds were true, but what was even more true about me was that I was rescued and beloved. I believed that in spite of the horrible things I had experienced, and the scarring choices I had made in my pain, that what God had in mind for my life was beautiful and right. It may not be of epic proportion compared to that of others' stories, but it would be my story, my pearl.

The summer before I graduated from high school I took a government class at a local college. I had never thought much about how government worked really. History was never my strong suit with all the dates and wars and names I couldn't keep organized. With the exception of wearing stickers for recent presidential candidates my mom loved, and advocating for social issues in marches, I didn't really pay attention to politics. I knew enough of what Scripture said on issues debated to see how the differing sides got their conclusions. I also knew that conflict was to be expected, that this world's inhabitants would never roll over and accept God's view of things, but would contradict His teaching at every turn, even the well-meaning ones. I trusted God created humanity and knew how it worked best, so I adopted beliefs on matters based on Scripture and left it at that. I saw Christians saying wise things, Christians saying cruel things, non-Christians saying wise things, non-Christians saying cruel things. I wanted to be a part of the conversation, but I wanted to be redemptive and didn't know how or if it was possible.

One day in that government class we watched the movie, "Mr. Smith Goes to Washington". I sat wide-eyed during the scene where he stands to filibuster, holding the floor and speaking out for what he believed was right with grit and determination in spite of the stuffy, deep-pocketed know-it-alls striving to shut him and his cause down. Something came alive in me during that scene. I knew what I was made for and that somehow I was going to hold a floor and speak for what I believed was right with grit and determination one day. I didn't know what a loud girl from the "wrong side of town" could talk about, or who would ever listen, but I tucked that dream away and trusted that if God meant for it, it would come about in the right time.

After all, He wasn't just skilled at diving, rescuing, healing and restoring. He was also masterful at setting the stage for His name to shine.

"For if you remain completely silent at this time, relief and deliverance will arise for the Jews from another place, but you and your father's house will perish. Yet who knows whether you have come to the kingdom for such a time as this?"

—ESTHER 4:14

God knew our stories before the first page was written. We are living stories within a God-sized story, and both are finished and yet unfolding. It is a mysterious wonder, but God's sovereignty—His supreme ultimate control—can stabilize us with comfort and inspire us with hope that nothing can keep us from being used in our generation.

We can easily look at the holes and drill marks in our shells, feel the scar tissue from wounds cut out by the saving hands of Jesus, and can wonder how in the world God could ever use us. We feel so far from finished, still capable of being bound up with burdens. We feel disqualified from epic, from being an essential role in God's bigger story. We are tempted to shrink away, hide the pearls, and settle for being saved. Being saved eternally is amazing, yes, but we forget our salvation, we forget Who saved us and why, and we forget that He is telling a bigger story, with us in it. Remembering daily that we are secure in a forever love and family regardless of how we look or act can energize us to keep stepping into the newness of life with Jesus. But how do we remember something we have forgotten?

Someone else usually has to remind us.

Esther was born in ancient Persia. Though God is not mentioned explicitly in the pages of her story, His presence is no less evident in her most defining moments. Orphaned as a child after the loss of her parents, heart-broken and disoriented, she was taken in and raised by an uncle, Mordecai. With no womanly influence, no married parents under her roof, and growing up on the "wrong side" of town as a Jew, Esther was an unlikely Queen of Persia. And yet, her setting fit her perfectly for the epic destiny God designed just for her. Whatever she learned from Mordecai, we know that humility, wisdom and faith in an unseen God was impressed upon her because she displayed these qualities from the moment her feet hit marble. God knew what her beginning would look like, what her burdens would be, and yet He opened doors for her to enter a palace to face a king. In her defining moment, when the history of God's people hung in the balance, God used Esther's story to bring salvation. For a few holy moments, a woman held a floor, spoke out for what she believed was right and the heavens and earth proclaimed God's fame.

She could have stayed silent. She could have denied the whisper of her epic calling. She could have hidden away in the safety of the palace walls. If she had she would have missed her grand destiny and in time would probably lose her own life.

But she didn't stay silent. She was reminded who she was and where she came from by someone who knew both God and her. Mordecai reminded her that she was where she was, in her palace setting, for a reason. She was orphaned, heartbroken, raised by him, Jewish, from the "wrong side" of town, and now chosen by the King of Persia, for a reason designed by the God of the Jews. Now, telling her story was the most appropriate brave next thing to do.

God used Esther's brave story-telling step. What could have brought shame and imminent death to her and many others instead became a glorious display of faith and courage that is celebrated and re-told by Jews and Gentiles to this day, thousands of years later. Though her life was spared and she continued to reign as Queen, had she lost her life God would have honor waiting for her just as He has promised for the many who have been martyred in His name.

There is a principle that runs through all of Scripture that is perhaps my favorite, and most hope-stirring anchor:

God has a pattern of using unlikely people to do unbelievable things.

For example, who could have ever imagined:

…a young slave girl influencing an enemy military leader so that he encounters and trusts in the one true God.

…a woman way beyond child-bearing age bearing a child and having descendants like the stars in the sky.

…a virgin woman bearing a child and giving birth to the prophesied Messiah, in spite of every obstacle.

…a baby being the promised King of the Jews and Redeemer of all humanity.

…a dead Jewish carpenter rising from the dead and appearing to many before ascending to the Father as the perfect sacrifice for all our sins.

…a murderer of Christians experiencing Christ for himself and then writing most of the New Testament, or,

...God bringing to pass redemption for Adam, Eve and the earth through one man, Jesus, and folding in Gentiles and Jews together into Christ's Kingdom fulfilling God's promise to Abraham and extending eternal grace to all through faith in Jesus!

God has a thing for the gnarled and clamped tight wounded, it would seem. His heart is bent on redeeming, and no challenge is too great for Him. No matter the depth, He can dive it. No matter the seal, He can pry it. No matter the burden, He can polish it. He can set our wounds, and then set our pearls, our stories of His redemption in our lives. We may feel like unlikelies, but God's track record is proof that the unbelievable is yet possible in our lives as we choose to surrender to Him in our generation.

MY REDEMPTION STORY

I was just a child in my faith when I was in college, but I began growing quickly as I discovered that God could be trusted with one broken area of my life after another. It was the first semester of my sophomore year, I was a pre-med major with a minor in music and I was falling apart at the seams. The relationship I thought was headed toward marriage painfully ended, at least temporarily. My dad was in jail and I was emotionally numbing with food and gaining weight in spite of medications I took all summer to shed unwanted pounds. In part because of the stress, I was failing both organic chemistry and biology and was on the fast track to academic probation. No matter how hard I tried to hold everything together, things just kept unraveling.

Oh, how blessed was that unraveling though.

At my end, I surrendered to God's way for everything, and what I found was a beginning again. What ended was Heather's way of forging a life of meaning, but in it was death for my soul.

What was born in that broken dream's place was God's way of freeing me to live a life of meaning that fits me in every way. God tenderly got low and close with me and reminded me of what I most enjoy doing, of when I am most alive. God reminded me of my dreams of being in His epic story doing something brave in a way that fits me. He reminded me of Mr. Smith in Washington, and of the trauma I had experienced as a child. He reminded me of feeling like I was a boy, of confusion, of shame, of secret sorrow. He reminded me of His rescue, His grace, His endless love. He reminded me of my love for words, for speaking and writing and being on a stage. With everything in me I sensed God say to my soul, "Heather, I gave you a mouth, and I'd like to use it."

God already had my heart, but in that moment I gave Him my mouth.

I was sitting in a little sandwich shop in the basement of LaFortune, a popular student center in the middle of the Notre Dame campus, when I first spoke the words out loud to a friend, "I just changed my major to Government & International Studies. God made me to use my words, He gave me a mouth and He wants to use it!" I even declared boldly that I'd be an advocate for others, even a Senator someday, and would speak for those who had no voice. I didn't know what I was talking about but I was filled with passion, and my hands were flailing with animation as I spoke from this place wide awake within me. I finally felt at home in my own soul and was overwhelmed by the awareness that God knew me and wanted to use me as-is, without me needing to be anyone else. It was during my inaugural speech in our booth when all of a sudden my arm crashed into the dangling light overhead, shattered it into a thousand pieces and sent the whole place into darkness. My friend and I sat stunned for a few seconds as we realized we were surprisingly unharmed. I was obviously and rightly humbled; I wanted to shatter strongholds on women's souls, not light bulbs. The irony was not lost on me that I could add to the darkness if my gifts were used to grow my name and not God's. But then grace prevailed and gave us belly laughs until we couldn't see to walk straight and had to walk hand-in-hand until we could walk up and out into the day.

God was calling me to look at the setting He had prepared for me, for my story, and to trust His plans for me. He was showing me on a high level at the time that the pieces of my story that seemed like mistakes, that I thought needed to be painted over, or thrown in a trash, were going to be put on display for His glory and my freedom. A year later I had a name plate that affirmed what I said in that booth that day. I had been elected by my peers to represent my Junior class on the most prestigious council on campus, and as I placed my name plate on the desk for our first meeting, I remembered that broken light and said a prayer before I opened my mouth. "Senator Heather DeJesus" was for me a beginning of a new epic adventure, where God designed my setting, and was about to put His work on display.

As I write this chapter news stations are reporting stories of sexual harassment popping up like a celebrity twitter feed. A dam has broken wide and women are speaking in the light about things that have been done in the dark, hiding their secrets in shame's shadow no longer. My heart has grieved for the women who have suffered in silence. I have felt ill for the families now experiencing shock, humiliation and turmoil. I have prayed for restoration for everyone involved, and for the friends and communities who are left in disbelief, now disoriented and mistrusting.

My heart has been heavy through all this because many years before I was married, I was in this same place of confronting an offender myself. Sexual harassment has a way of drawing out all the places in us we try to ignore, all the fears and doubts about who we are and why we are here. We are surprised to find a serpent in the Garden, an irritant in the waters, a wounded and wounding person in the workplace. There we are going about our business hoping for a thousand wonderful things to happen in our lives, dismissing the doubts and shouts that we are never going to amount to anything; when all of a sudden an inappropriate exchange takes place. We didn't see the situation coming. We discount it because of all the doubts and shouts inside. We think there's no way we could be right and they could be wrong. Then through their words, suggestions, and unwanted advances they prey on our hallmark asset: our vulnerability. To be vulnerable is not necessarily being naïve, or weak, or unwise even. Being vulnerable can actually be brave. To show up and be who you are without apology, without pretense, authentic and accessible, able to receive goodness from others and give from a solid place to others is one of the loveliest qualities healthy women possess. Certainly womanhood also brings with it grit as much as tenderness, competency as well as compassion, depth as well as delight. But to be vulnerable in today's world of social media backlash, bullies, stalkers and those who seek to strike terror in our neighborhoods, it takes a gut-full of gumption to show up as-is, believing that what you bring to the table is enough and that God can use you and will fill your gaps as needed. Our vulnerability, our willingness to show up to our lives and be who God says we are trusting that this is enough, has the potential to free generations of women who may otherwise be bound in shame. Is it any wonder then why the irritant would come against women in such a destructive and shaming way?

Within months of my harassment experience, a door was opened for me to receive free therapeutic support. I brought my recent pain to the light and with it came all the pain in my story. The very thing designed to derail me actually propelled me into deeper healing and wider hope for my future. Finally, the heartache of my childhood traumas found clean air through confession, and God guided me through the pain I wasn't able to fully feel as a child. As I felt the grief, cried the tears, processed the anger and resentment, I found a wide place opening up within me of acceptance. I couldn't go back and remove the hurts from my past, I couldn't undo the damage, or change the script, but God took me to the rooms of my past and showed me where He had been standing and how He saw me in that space. He showed me how He had been with me all along, enduring the pain with me, grieving with me, and was at work already in that room preparing something beautiful for me. I wasn't alone, in His eyes I was lovely, and now more than ever I was better able to use my voice to offer hope to women who were still stuck in those rooms surrounded by fear and shame.

Since that time God has used my voice to reach women of diverse backgrounds with Gospel hope, from northeast Tennessee and Washington D.C., to Guatemala, Peru and a remote Amazon village in Brazil. For a season I was able to speak up for and into the lives of women who live on the edge of homelessness and helped launch a restorative ministry that funnels women into a healing journey within a home environment.

God used my voice to serve the former Governor of Florida, Jeb Bush, during the heartbreaking Terri Schiavo case in 2005. Recruited as an attorney to work alongside a select team of professionals, we worked with humble urgency to research and advise leadership how to best exercise the state's interest in protecting the dignity of human life.

God used my voice to inform elected officials in the Florida House of Representatives of legislative rules and procedures so as to effectively serve the citizens of Florida during former Speaker Marco Rubio's administration.

God used my voice to help sustain the life of a handicapped child facing imminent death because the single mother had a low income and couldn't garner the support for medical expenses.

God used my voice to educate local women how to lobby Congress on matters that violate their conscience, showing them how to go office to office in D.C., using their voices to impact change.

God uses my voice to share Gospel hope with women of different generations, but also through a mentoring ministry reaching vulnerable kids in our community, through our family business and through my role as an Ambassador for Noonday Collection where we are together "building a flourishing world where children are cherished, women are empowered, people have jobs and we are connected"[48].

In my most cherished roles, I am yielding my voice to God as a wife, filling my man's soul with encouraging truth and cheerleading him into his destiny. And as a mama, I get to shape my daughter's perception of God, herself, and her world through the words and stories I choose. I cannot imagine a more precious audience, a more critical message, or a more privileged platform than right here, in my home.

I have certainly experienced seasons of silence though; this has not been a smooth path by any means. My voice has been quieted in times of brokenness over my own sin, or when grief has become indescribable. In times of transition I find my voice gets shaky, grasps for hope and needs space to reattach to our sovereign God and remember who is holding all the things together. One of these silent seasons has been recent. For two years after stepping down from vocational ministry, my voice was quiet and limited to a few friends and family, shared texts, confessions, and simple gatherings in homes. The quiet space was needed as we fostered for a time and I walked further through infertility grief and a fear of loss after experiencing some trauma with adoption. In the silence I anchored my worth again in the person of Jesus Christ and not in what I contribute to the world or how I'm perceived by others. My voice was not silent before God, and I could hear Him speak to me as well. I found healing in being accepted in obscurity, that I don't "have" to speak up for anyone, or for any cause to be worth something. I considered that speaking to my family and a few friends may be my primary purpose in life, and that satisfaction comes in fulfilling our purpose no matter the scale or scope. Ultimately, I trusted that if God wanted to use me in other ways, He would simply make a way.

In the summer of 2017, it would seem He was making a way. I remember the day, it was in June, and I was headed to meet with a counseling friend. Something had been stirring in me for weeks; I couldn't explain it except that I felt restless. It was as if I was rubbing up against the cocoon walls I had been contained in for two years. I had abandoned a blog and most of my social media outlets except for Instagram and was chomping at the bit to post about some of the observations I was making in my inner life. My friend affirmed the health in my stirrings and desire, so fueled with a little courage I posted from that loved place after our meeting. With that one post on Instagram I could almost hear the crack of my cocoon! I felt something give way inside and I knew the season of silence had passed. It was time for me to speak again. I wasn't sure where or how or on what, but I had blood flowing back to my voice. What I never expected was for an old colleague in publishing, who was now the president of a publishing company, to contact me after seeing that one post and offer me a contract to publish my first book! Truly, God uses unlikely people to do amazing things, and I think He especially gets a kick out of giving loud girls from the "wrong side of town" book deals when they just want to talk about His Gospel.

Yet I still almost said no. At the thought of writing a book—which was a dream of mine coming true—I immediately was overcome by fear and shame. Naturally I felt fear of being exposed to people who could want to harm me, but I also felt fear of just being known as I am. Shame reminded me that I am "wordy" and that people have been telling me that all my life. In a deep way I have tried to "edit" myself before presenting myself in relationship or professionally. If I could just lighten the weight I bring in passion and words, maybe I'd be acceptable. It was not until the actual editing process of this book that God brought me a revelation, a new way to embrace the way He has made me. On a quiet retreat in Saint Augustine, Florida, I put my computer down on a bed and got on my knees, beaten down by the heavy hits with the word "wordy" telling me I had no right to write. The softest whisper lanced my heart with this response:

I enjoy your wordiness.

It never occurred to me in all my years that God could enjoy something about me others rejected. I could feel the tent pegs of other self-rejecting thoughts losing their grip on my soul. If it was true that God enjoyed me AS-IS, then I could show up to my life. In fact, the only way I can show up to my life is if I first believe God enjoys the wordy, the nerdy and the weird. And on that floor on my knees in Saint Augustine, He assured me He does.

As women who have the Creator residing within us, with a mission to subdue and rule and multiply, we are to work against the injustices of our generation. Where there is verbal and physical abuse of women, we should be there. Where there is a degradation of women through pornography we should be reaching those women, loving them, speaking out against this assault on womanhood. Where there are attitudes suggesting women are of less value or worth than men, we should be prayerfully using our influence to reset them. However, this work is not to be done through usurping God's authority. God is the only one who defines what is good. He is the author of identity, not us. God is the one who chooses our setting, not us. He set us in our bodies, in our clusters, in our generation, and He is intentional about every detail, down to the last freckle. The irritant would love to work us up into a frothy mess trying to redefine all the terms according to our own creative design, removing the boundaries God set for our good.[49] This is the way that has been suggested since the beginning of time, and is filling our ears in our generation, but we have God's power in us to resist this tide. The diver and the farmer, they know what they are doing. They have rescued us, removed our burdens, and have set us in this place, with these hard stories, in our generation. For such a time as this we can share our redemptive stories, our pearls, and point to our God and Redeemer. We will be agents of change but in God's way, centering always and only on the Gospel of Jesus Christ and not on any other gospel.

And all the women said, A{wo}men.

DISCUSSION QUESTIONS
10—THE SETTING

YOUR REDEMPTION STORY

Did you ever imagine that you were born and raised where you were, when you were, by whom you were, on purpose for a purpose?

_____

_____

_____

How can you see your personal setting, your cluster, your privileges and your challenges growing up working together as a preparation for your unique calling? (For people with histories of severe trauma, this may not be easy to see so please don't force it. Pray instead for God to continue to reveal His love for you and in time, His redemptive plans.)

_____

_____

_____

OTHER REDEMPTIVE STORIES

Describe a time when you thought to yourself, "This is it. This is what I'm made for..."

_____

_____

_____

Not all of us will stand bravely before a king, like Esther, but all of us are called to our own brave moments. Share one of yours.

_____

_____

_____

Consider this quote: "God has a pattern of using unlikely people to do unbelievable things." Share an example of when you felt like an "unlikely" person to do something, and why you felt unlikely. How did God do it through you?

_____

_____

_____

Have you embraced God's enjoyment of you in your unique design? What is your "wordy" and what could happen if you believed God enjoys even this about you?

_____

_____

_____

11

the Best Care Practices

"I shall ask into my shell only those friends with whom I can be completely honest. I find I am shedding hypocrisy in human relationships. What a rest that will be. The most exhausting thing in life, I have discovered, is being insincere."
—ANNE MORROW LINDBERGH[50]

I heard the farmer and diver talking softly about my pearl. Apparently pearls are tougher than they appear, but they aren't invincible. Water, air and light weren't concerns for them, they were made for the elements. But there are toxins that can eat away at their luster, could dull them, could cause harm. I was so relieved the farmer knew what he was doing. I felt pretty clueless about caring for this precious little living one born from my affliction. Others may not see the struggle behind their shine, but I remember. I know the sleepless nights that went into those layers, the thin hope and simple trust in the diver.

I sure hope my pearl is handled well, she is now priceless to me. I can tell she is of highest value to the farmer and diver too, after all...they staked their lives, and set their name, upon us.

The oyster does nothing in the harvesting process, except breathe and respond to the work of the diver and farmer as they use precision tools to create a new story. This is the grace of God displayed, a receiving of care, rescue, cleansing and restoration. No one would ever expect the oyster to try to surface on her own, try to open and spit out the embedded mass woven into her flesh, or try to repurpose her wounding. This would be ridiculous, and a viral YouTube wonder if it were to ever be captured!

For those of us of the human variety, our harvesting process also depends entirely on the grace of God, as does our life-long restoration process too. The difference is that we actually get to partner with God in the restoration process as we actively engage with truth set out in God's Word. As God exposes lies we are believing, and we exchange our thoughts for the truth God gives us, we can watch as our wounds that were designed to destroy us instead become the stage for God's fame in our healing. But this faith work is more than just rewiring our minds, it is a real every day tending of our souls. Learning to nurture, nourish and cherish the Spirit of God within us is our part in God's grand display. As we share our redemptive stories, we learn to walk in humility, to stay in step with God's Spirit through prayer, and to exercise wisdom over when and how we share God's love and truth through our stories. We are also lovingly taught to grow up into mature adults who learn how to guard our souls against the corrosive nature of our flesh and the destructive ways of the world in which we live.

Jewel experts give similar basic instructions on how to best care for pearls. As organic gems, (they are living), they require special care to sustain them for a long time. As any living thing, too, they can be harmed or used poorly.

We all want lives with luster, not shiny and artificial, but rich and authentic and solid in the middle, glowing with glory. No one goes into their life hoping that in the end they hold up something that looks ragged, tested and found to be of imitation quality. But we get to choose how we invest in our souls, the place that generates our living redemptive stories with God. If we will heed instruction and make the space and time to nourish them, the goodness of God displayed in our stories can be passed down for generations!

So, here are some basic care instructions for real living pearls:

- They can be harmed by contact with any chemicals found in everyday items, like household cleaners and beauty products.
- Only clean your pearl with water and mild natural soap. Use nothing containing vinegar, some ammonias, chlorine, or bleach which will harm your pearls.
- Use a soft damp cloth to clean your pearl, never abrasive materials such as toothbrushes or scouring pads.
- Never leave your pearls around direct sources of heat, not intentionally.
- As organic materials, they need a little moisture so they don't dry out. Never store them in an extremely dry room or safety deposit box.
- Store them in a soft cloth or in a pouch to protect them from abrasive objects.
- If dripped on, soak in lukewarm water and mild natural soap. Rinse and dry.
- Wearing your pearls will return some oils from your skin to the pearls. The pH of your sweat can damage pearls, so it is best to remove them before undertaking any sweat-inducing activity.

Non-abrasive, no scouring, soft, gentle, away from direct sources of heat, don't dry them out, put them on last after you have put on all the stuff that makes you, well, you.

Pearls and acid never mix well. The nacre of a pearl, that luminous substance pearls are made of, contains some organic proteins and calcium carbonate which dissolves when it comes into contact with acid. Even mild acids take their toll over time, and when you're caring for a gem that is passed along to others for generations, limiting or avoiding exposure to acid is important.

As pearls and acid never mix well, one destroying the other, so too our redemptive stories and shame never mix well. Before we share our redemptive stories, we are wise to first put on truth about who we are and be set for the day in the confidence of Christ. If we don't, if we put on our redemptive stories first and tell others where we've been, what has happened, what Jesus did, we run the risk of exposing our living stories to the acid of shame through someone's bad day or bad life, a misunderstanding or judgment, or the relentless onslaught of the irritant constantly accusing us of being wanna-be women, and so on.

Just as acid exposure causes pearls to lose their gorgeous luster, and leads to a cloudy and dull appearance, our souls too can dim when we are regularly exposed to shame, lies and the brutality of sin at work in and around us. Our precious and tender places, our heartaches restored by the love of God, are hearty and can withstand much wear and tear. Over time though, the exposure to the acid of this life without rinsing, without drying, will lead us to the need for repair through an intensive polishing process. And in some cases, the erosion from continual contact with acids can result in some serious altering.

Dissolved, dulled, disfigured.

I find it interesting too that the most dangerous killers of precious pearls are found in the everyday beautification activities we engage in on a daily basis. Most damaged pearls are victims of the various acids that make up our personal grooming products: our perfumes, our lotions, hairsprays, and make-up. I find this telling, as a woman, since shame comes in hot and lethal for me through the lens of womanhood, and in particular regarding my femininity and appearance. I'm not saying stop using these products but be mindful of how they break down your pearls, and how the pursuit of outward beauty can weaken the luster of our security in a self-worth that is solid and unchanging, only being renewed as we grow older with Jesus.

Exposed over time, the pearl nacre breaks down, reducing it to a tiny disconnected blob. Minus the tiny, I can relate to disconnected blob. At the company Pearls International, they use a method for cleaning called a "dip-and-swirl" method where they fill a bowl with pearl-friendly cleanser, drop the pearl in and gently swirl it for about thirty seconds, alternating the direction occasionally to ensure all the nooks and crannies are sufficiently cleansed of the acidic oils.[51]

Dip and swirl.

Herein lies our hope for the inevitable wear down of our soul's strand of pearls. Call it our instructions, our best care practices to retain our luster:

Sabbath.

"Jesus said to them, `Come away with me. Let us go alone to a quiet place and rest for a while.'"

—MARK 6:31[52]

God's Holy Spirit takes up residence within us the moment we place our trust in Christ. When Jesus said, "It is finished" on His cross, He said it about us at the moment of our salvation. It is finished. Nothing can separate us from the love of God; not our sin, not our shame, not others' sins against us, not death or spiritual attack, physical distance, light or dark. Nothing means nothing. We are safe in the eternal security of Christ's blood shed for us, and on that basis alone are we confident of our hope of Heaven with Him. But our lives in the here and now can look and feel very different from what God desires for us if we believe lies about ourselves and expose ourselves to unbiblical toxins designed to wear our souls down.

This wearing down of our souls is why we are called to remove ourselves from the noise and hustle of this life to periodically and intentionally "dip and swirl" in the goodness of God.

Sabbath was created for God first; I forget this. He wanted to pause and enjoy all the good He already made, before moving forward with more. Enough is enough when we take the time to look at what has already been done and honor the work with attention and gratitude. If God Himself needed to dip and swirl for a space of time in His own goodness, how much more do we need this space?

Remove.
Dip.
Swirl.

And do this periodically.

It is foolish to neglect this; we will not sustain the health and vitality of our souls unless we apply these best practices. There is no other way, all other ways to shine only break us down, thin our souls and cause us to bubble into disconnected blobs.

May it not be so with our souls.

MY REDEMPTION STORY

As a teenager, I knew nothing of my soul's needs. Nothing means nothing. I knew I needed to brush my teeth, exercise, eat lean meats, be satisfied with the portion I was given, do my homework, follow the rules, treat others like I wanted to be treated, and so on. I knew what to do to care well for my body and form healthy friendships, not that I did this mind you. I knew how to read books, and later I learned how to understand God's Word, and discern quality teachers and messages. Not that I did this all the time either. But as for my soul, I didn't really even understand that I had one until my 20s. I kept the noise up high in my life constantly: TV, music, friends, activities, fixing, working, anything to keep from experiencing silence and solitude. So if it wasn't for pain resurrecting from my childhood traumas, I may have never discovered the richest gift God offers us as His children.

At 21 when I called off my prior engagement, I prayed that God would block me from any guy who would ultimately be a "Mr. Right Now". I wanted to keep my heart steady until my Mr. Right showed up. Had I known it would be 10 years, I may have adjusted my prayer a bit to make space for some date nights and hand holding, but hindsight is 20/20.

It was within the wrapping of singleness that God packaged one of His greatest gift to me as a daughter. My 20s were marked by education, travel, world-wide experiences, marathons, careers, big cities, beach towns, deep friendships, hard cries, and an invitation to know Jesus intimately like I had never imagined was possible. It was in my 20s when I learned about the inner life, that there is a relationship God wants to grow between us that takes place mostly in the unseen quiet place between Him and our soul. I discovered that He meets with us in the flesh through others He resides in, and also breathes the air with me in the solitude of a shared space, alone and yet together. I reconciled with silence, and found that I love it, and even crave it. I read the Word, over and over, and it became so familiar to me it eventually became my only real comfort in times of distress. I found my name in my 20s, because though I knew what my name meant, "little flower", I didn't see myself this way. Far from it. But God wooed me in my single years and showed me how He sees me, that to Him I am His little flower. I found contentment in being unknown, obscure, and without a throng around me at all times. In fact, His attention became all I wanted on some days. Toward the end of my 20s my friends knew that Monday nights were my "date nights". {Prepare yourself to roll your eyes or cynically laugh and decide that I am officially whacko. It's ok, I've gotten over it.} On those nights I was unavailable for dinner or hanging out, because I was going to be with Jesus, intentionally listening, paying attention, talking and sharing just between us. I was detaching from my constant need for others to validate who I am as a person and was learning to attach to my Creator.

I joined a local church and became active in forming community with others. As I deepened in accountability and mutual friendship, I noticed a love forming in me for the local church and could see how Jesus could love the Church and call her His bride. I had been carrying "church wounds" from childhood too, and during this season God showed me how the people who fill the seats are the Church, not the building, but that God would be faithful to use the local church to spread His Gospel to the end. I was finally able to accept the humanity of His Church and still see His goodness too.

Some of the deep friendships became mentoring relationships, where I was the mentee. I learned how to practice basic soul care and I was introduced to "quiet retreats" as a way to pull away from the constant pushing in my life. These consisted of guided readings, a schedule with breaks to rest, read, pray and eat, all within a 24-36 period of complete silence. Without fail, I would leave these times calmer on the inside, with a renewed awareness of my acceptance by God, as well as a desire for more communication with Him in my daily life. I also began practicing the Scripture-reading method *lectio divina*, which is slow and intentional—two characteristics that had not been present in my life up to this point. As I started to pay more attention to the Person of God with me, Jesus, the Word became a joy and a comfort, rather than a book full of rules. I joined and began leading Bible studies as a natural consequence of my growing love for Jesus' presence in my life, and I believe this slow daily chewing of the Word for years is the reason I have any sincerely good works to show for my life.

All of it was a practice in relationship, a learning of how to be myself with someone else who sees me as I really am and accepts me fully. Sabbath was not about taking time *off* but about choosing time *with* a God who is always seeking to reveal more of Himself to us. My single years with God were the greatest gift. In a sense, it was the parenting I needed, the friendship I wanted, the marriage I longed for, and the companionship I would need forever.

And it all came to me through the gift of pain, born of trauma. My soul finding rest was a treasure I wanted but I didn't know it existed. Had I not been cut, had there been no wounding, no irritating rub...there would have been no pearl.

Growing up doesn't guarantee we won't feel sorrow deeply, or suffer emotional heartache ever again, in fact it is the opposite. For those who follow Jesus, growing up means we expect pain to come and move in life anyway, expecting God to provide all we need. Our expectation of goodness to come from our suffering is not based on some wishful feel-good positive attitude we wear on a t-shirt, but on the resurrected Christ who defeated every force of evil on His cross.

"These things I have spoken to you, that in Me you may have peace. In the world you will have tribulation; but be of good cheer, I have overcome the world."

—JOHN 16:33

We feel pain in life because we progressively stop trying to constantly avoid it out of fear. We learn to trust that God is in control and is purposing something for us through the suffering. We feel the pain, and maybe feel it even more deeply because we are feeling love, joy, and peace more deeply as well. It is as if our nerve endings are more sensitive emotionally because we are more fully awake to our lives, and feeling pain deeply is just one of the proofs that we are alive. Feeling our emotions is not easy though. My greatest courage may be feeling my life. And not everyone is a deep feeler like me. Certainly some suffer but in their own way that seems less intense to others. Pain like love, though, is personal and valid no matter how it is experienced by a person.

Just as we grow physically, we grow spiritually, and emotionally, and some seasons we grow slowly, while at other times we seem to shoot straight into the sky! Our souls are complex, and much is hidden from our conscience. This too requires us to put our faith in Jesus to do for us what we cannot do for ourselves. Just as we cannot make our hearts to beat, or our neurons to fire, we trust God to make known what needs our attention. And then, when He allows for something to flare up and cause us distress, it is wise for us to proceed with caution.

I shared earlier about a time not too long ago when I stepped down from vocational ministry. It was one of the hardest decisions I have had to make because I loved the mission behind what I did. I felt most at home in that career than any I had ever felt before, though there were aspects that didn't fit me at all. For many reasons, becoming a women's ministry leader felt like a dream come true; it let me exercise my spiritual passion more than practicing law did at least. Me even getting the job had God's hand all over it, so when I sensed Him nudging me to quit so I could rest and heal, it felt like I was kissing a dream good-bye. Thankfully, I learned in my 20s to pay attention to my soul and seek God's wisdom when I noticed signals that there were problems within.

When we learned we were a part of the "unexplained infertility" community, I was on staff at our church and was largely overseeing "mother" ministries of some kind. All my friends in the community my age were having children, or already had children, and baby bumps seemed to be on every other social media post. I sincerely felt like I was processing infertility grief as authentically and healthily as I could, but it wasn't until we had our beautiful daughter through adoption, brought her home and then began experiencing a deteriorating relationship with some of her biological people that I really started to face infertility grief, and fear, head on. In spite of every effort to build a bridge, we faced a separation we did not initiate. As the situation continued to unravel, we were eventually confronted with the need to seek legal protection. The heartache of losing ties to my daughter's biological roots, of losing connection with someone I deeply cared for and wanted the best for, of constant assault that stirred up fear of being harmed or of losing our daughter—crippled me. Shame told me I failed this person, failed my daughter, failed my family, failed for all adoptive families and failed Jesus. Shame told me I had no business ministering to women. I couldn't even minister to this one person. Shame was sounding more and more like the true story, and I knew it was time to take a step back. I knew there was pressure in me that needed to release in a safe place, and with the encouragement and persistence of my husband I quit.

This girl needed to remove, dip and swirl.

I didn't have any plans for a next career, I had a beautiful toddler at home I was thrilled to spend my energy on, and immediately called to set up counseling sessions to work through infertility grief and post-adoptive trauma. For a while I wanted nothing to do with anyone. I pulled away from every social commitment I once held, stepped away from every leader-ish position, and became a recluse. The only thing I did was eat dinner with other moms by adoption, and even then I fought back tears through the meal. Days turned into weeks, and weeks into months until one night I looked at Jonathan and told him I wanted to host a gathering. Just one night though, not a regular thing. He seemed relieved. He said, "the whole 'I'm burrowing into a hole and taking you both with me' thing was a little scary." Then he suggested something I thought was completely ridiculous. He told me I should start selling for Noonday Collection. I say this was ridiculous because I'm not a business-minded type of person, that's all him. And, I was living off the grid. I was not blogging anymore, I was hardly on social media, and I was afraid to use my name. He continued to nudge me back to my passion though, reminding me that God placed in me a desire to speak and use my voice to share the Gospel and stir hope up in women's hearts. I also wore accessories from Noonday Collection often so since he had pretty much already invested in their seasonal collections, I think he figured he could recoup some of it if I became an Ambassador! I squirmed, I laughed it off and spent the next few days debating over whether it was absurd or brilliant. Less than a week later I was meeting with a friend to finish a study on emotional recovery when I read this verse found in Isaiah 58:10:

"If you extend your soul to the hungry
And satisfy the afflicted soul,
Then your light shall dawn in the darkness,
And your darkness shall be as the noonday."

My soul had felt darkness and longed for the light but digging into a hole and hiding away in my wound and fear was not the path to healing. Using my voice to bring hope to artisans stepping out of poverty around the world, using my voice to encourage women in my community in living rooms and kitchens, this was not just the way of Noonday Collection, it was the path God was guiding me on for my own noonday story.[53]

My expectations were low and I made sure Jonathan's were too. He gave me permission to simply enjoy it, and not earn

$1. I may have honored that blessing with all my purchases! I determined with every door God opened I would share three stories: (1) an artisan's story, (2) God's redemption story, and (3) my story. As I used my voice to do God's pleasure, I realized that I shared more in common with our artisan partners than I first noticed. We were both experiencing poverty but for me it was of an emotional nature. Together though we were experiencing hope and restored joy as we crossed a bridge secured by Christ's love and our dignified work with Noonday Collection. I walked out of my poverty of soul into marvelous light alongside my new sisters and brothers through Noonday. Our neediness was a bridge, our hope was a bridge, our work was a bridge, and together we were connected.

As an Ambassador for Noonday Collection I also discovered a truth that has helped shape the focus of this book! With each trunk show and with each presentation I made I could feel a broken place inside me mend just a little more. As I used my voice to share the redemption of God and the redeeming hope of dignified work for men and women around the world, I was experiencing redemption in my wounds as well. The pain of shame was being washed away as I dipped and swirled in the rest of God, in the sufficiency of Jesus' cross to make me whole, and as I served out of my giftings. Telling my story and having women listen and respond with empathy stitched my soul back into a new and lovely shape. I would never be the same as I was before the grief and trauma, but my new normal was becoming filled with life too.

Now that I look back I see another key hidden in Isaiah 58:10: IF. I had a choice in my pain, a choice to look at my pain only or to look to God as my Healer and simply move on loving others in a way that fit me. As I trusted God with my pain and sought to do what little I could to "satisfy the afflicted soul" I not only found light again, but I found my voice.

Had I not paid attention to the warning signs in my soul to slow down, to pull over, to stop, I would have missed all this. I could have persisted in the working of ministry, but I would have missed my own recovery. And this is a continuation process, the recovery never fully ends, but ebbs and flows. The Sabbath cycles, it isn't one and done, it is here, and there, and here again. It is a practice in relationship, a learning of how to be myself with someone else who sees me as I really am and accepts me fully.

We remove, we dip, and we swirl, and only then can we shine on.

DISCUSSION QUESTIONS
11—THE BEST CARE PRACTICES

YOUR REDEMPTION STORY

What did you know about your soul when you trusted in Christ?

_____

_____

_____

How does it feel to know God doesn't just care about your salvation, or your witness of Him, but that He deeply cares and concerns Himself with every detail of your life, including all you need?

_____

_____

_____

OTHER REDEMPTIVE STORIES

How has shame worked against your joy in being a human, in your relationship with your body, with others and with God?

_____

_____

_____

What does Sabbath look like for you? How do you remove, dip and swirl periodically? Has it changed as you've grown in your relationship with God?

_____

_____

_____

the Splendor of the Story

"One generation shall praise Your works to another,
And shall declare Your mighty acts.
On the glorious splendor of Your majesty
And on Your wonderful works, I will meditate.
Men shall speak of the power of Your awesome acts,
And I will tell of Your greatness...."
—PSALM 145:5-6, NASB

You may not know this about oysters. I didn't even realize it until the farmer explained it to me recently. Oysters have a regenerating way about them. They can filter the water they are in, prevent erosion, guard coasts from storm damage and oyster reefs can provide habitat for other organisms. In a beautifully literal way, oysters leave the deep in better shape than we found it.

For the first time in my life, I see myself as more than just a lump of tissue stuck in a rock of carbonite. I too have a destiny. I'm made for more than just sitting around taking up space, I'm an agent of change. As weak and small as I feel most days, the truth is I'm built for this.

Now I'm not going to lie, I'm still afraid of what could happen to me in the deep. What happened to me already was terrible, but I hear other stories of other cuts and drillings that sound worse than what I have experienced. But the difference between the fear I feel now and the fear I felt when I was first in the deep, is that now I know I'm seen. I'm loved. I'm known, and the pain I experience can be healed. I have something bigger than my fear to cling to now: the hope of my diver being always close to me ready to rescue just in the right time, the hope of my suffering being redeemed, and the hope of having a redemptive purpose in the deep. I don't have to go back, I want to go back. A time will come when I'll age out of this opportunity to serve in the deep, so for now I do what I can, what I'm made to do. I'm no martyr though. I'm not "taking one for the team" by being submerged back into these dangerous unpredictable waters. There's something in it for me! With every cut that comes my way, an opportunity forms along with new nacre, and the layers of faith in the diver's ability to redeem my hurt bring me comfort even in my discomfort. It isn't easy, in fact, it feels downright miserable at times, but the pearls that come from it...they are oh so lovely! And the farmer promises me he is collecting them for me, that someday, in some way, I will be able to enjoy endless pleasure and delight with him as I discover that all my afflictions will be displayed as all the wild pearls.

There is a word I learned in my 20s that became a breath prayer, a word I said under my breath and usually in a slow exhale daily.

Maranatha. Come, Lord Jesus.

The word "Maranatha" is Aramaic and means, "the Lord is coming". In the time of the early Church, when followers of Jesus faced severe persecution for submitting to one God, who was not Caesar, the term was a comforting reminder that the Messiah would usher in shalom, "peace", for them. It became a common greeting for believers in Jesus, even replacing "shalom" in Jewish practice. The Jews understood covenant promises, they knew Jews would become a nation of people, would have a government system established and would see Jesus, the Messiah, crowned as King of His Kingdom. This focus on future deliverance sustained them even through martyrdom as the time for Christ's Kingdom was yet to come.

There were many days in my 20s as I was processing childhood pain, as I was working through loneliness in singleness, as I was discerning my purpose and growing in my knowledge of God, when I grew weary of it all. The days felt long, the battles seemed constant and challenges appeared insurmountable. I remember looking out of the window in my car many times praying through my tears, *Maranatha*, just come now Jesus, take me home. The Jews said it to build up faith in one another, to cheer one another on in making disciples of Christ in deeply adverse conditions. I was using the word because I wanted out. I wanted done with this walk and was waving the white flag of surrender. As sweet as my relationship with Jesus was becoming in that space of time, my experiences in life and losses were wearing away at my soul and I saw very little hope of goodness outweighing the sadness in the future. My focus was admittedly on my comfort, my enjoyment, my pleasure in the here and now, and even though I knew God used my voice to encourage others with Gospel hope at times, I didn't see how I had any regenerating purpose in being here, or that there was something in it for me to plant and root while I'm here.

I prayed for God to lift my soul, lift my eyes, lift my vision so that I could see what He saw in my story, so I could hope and aim for something purposeful. I longed for meaning in suffering, for redemption of every single ache in my heart, for a story that would live on longer than me. I didn't know how God would answer those prayers, or if they would even be answered. But I got bolder, and I asked too that God would multiply me, a lonely single girl from the "wrong side of town". I prayed He would use my voice and would multiply my family in quality and in quantity. I prayed for purpose, for legacy, for rich meaning to come from my one life lived. I didn't see a husband on the horizon, in fact, I saw my family shrinking down to less than a handful. I didn't see influence flowing from my voice, in fact, I was in counseling, and felt disqualified to share encouragement to others. But now a couple of decades later, I see answers coming to those prayers. I see a woman surrounded, not just with a family growing in quality and quantity, but with vision and purpose.

I didn't meet Jonathan until 2008. I was 30 years old and had just bought my first house three months earlier. We lived states away and met through eHarmony, but having lived intentionally with God through our 20s, we were well able to recognize His hand at work in our relationship quickly and were married the same year we met! Our courtship was short, but we weaved it tightly within our communities, and our wedding was a celebration of those communities that nourished us during our formidable years. The prayer of my heart for our family to grow in quality and quantity became the prayer of both of our hearts in marriage, especially when we began the road of infertility.

As painful as infertility was, and still can be, God used a closed womb to open my heart to a vision for motherhood I may have never captured had I birthed a child. In my 30s I learned more about the reality of Heaven, and the future coming for those of us who put our trust in Jesus for salvation. What I once assumed would be boring, with us singing and sitting around all the time, was actually far from the truth. Scripture points us to a Kingdom with an economy, government, industry, satisfying labor, rich fellowship, and purposeful enterprise. All of this without the corruption of the flesh nature or sinful devices of an irritant.

A new beginning, a new Garden, a fresh start.

But better than the first, because we will have the redeemed stories of believers, we will have all the treasures of faith recovered in the fire of testing. We have never seen something as amazing as what is coming, and we can take an active part in how amazing it will actually be for us as individuals. Scripture calls them rewards, but they are the motivation for why we keep dwelling in the deep with God, why we walk with Jesus in hard places, why we persevere in our faith when we are already sealed and safe in the security of God's love. The Kingdom coming, the rewards being stored up on our behalf in addition to the bliss of being with God in perfection—this is what's "in it for us"!

As the reality of rewards began to dawn on me, I started evaluating all my commitments in terms of their eternal worth. I joked once that if I could I would create a device that would gong when I was attempting something that was completely worthless for eternity yet ding loudly when I was in the middle of something that really mattered. An "eternal-o-meter" if you will. But I actually don't need to invent this because God has already provided this for us. The Word provides a guide for living a meaningful life. As we take it in each day, and pray and seek God's wisdom and way for us, we discern what is good. With practice, we grow in sensitivity to the nudges of God's Holy Spirit who encourages us and warns us of fruitless endeavors. Our desire for healthy companionship grows and God's community of other recovering believers serves as a safe place to share stories, learn and heal. The Holy Spirit, the Word of God and the Body of Christ together form for us this "eternal-o-meter". We can also rest assured we will fulfill our purpose in the here and now, not because we get all this right, but because God is faithful to complete the work He started in us and in the whole world.

I realized that in the here and now I have a work to do. I have a regenerating purpose. If I live into my 90s I dream about attending as many weddings as I do funerals because of the relationships I continue to pour myself into. My purpose is not about performing to earn love or worth, it is to believe Jesus is who He says He is and live my life based on that belief. Jesus says Himself that:

"This is the work of God, that you believe in Him whom He has sent."

—JOHN 6:29

Believing in Jesus is our part in our redemption story, and in our redemptive stories. God will not do this part for us, it is our response to His work in love.

Believing in Jesus is simple for salvation, and sufficient. The same is true for all our trials after salvation; belief is simple. But it is far from easy. We have an irritant bent on drilling into our minds doubts and fears to erode our faith. If he cannot wear our faith down into fear, he will try to inflate our view of ourselves, boosting our confidence in ourselves to "do this" life thing on our own. He cannot keep us from God's secure love; we belong now to Him forever. But what he can and will do is try to keep us from fulfilling our regenerating purpose in this life. He will haunt us with fearful stories of cuts, of attacks, of failure, of futility, he will remind us of the beauty in the shallow, the ease, the comfort. He will tell us to cry, "Take me home Lord" so we don't stir up one another in faith for the hard places.

Believing Jesus in the deep, in suffering, in times when we feel abandoned, when shooters terrorize crowds of people below enjoying a concert, takes faith like a child. We simply believe Jesus is who He says He is, and that He is coming.

Maranatha. The Lord is coming. Take courage, persevere, dwell in the deep, share your stories, do good and enjoy God here, now.

"And behold, I am coming quickly, and My reward is with Me, to give to every one according to his work. I am the Alpha and Omega, the Beginning and the End, the First and the Last."

—REVELATION 22:12-13

If the doctrine of rewards is taught at all, it is at times taught in the context of the Judgment Seat of Christ and can easily be misunderstood because of the word "judgment" that is used when translating from Greek. As believers in Christ through faith, our assurance of salvation is secure. We do not have wrath any longer in our future. Though interpretations of Scripture surrounding the Judgment or Bema Seat of Christ vary, what is consistent with the Gospel and other Scriptures is that no punishment is meted out during this time upon the believer in Christ. This is a place of examination more for reward for living in step with Christ in this life. Though there is a time of "regret" implied in some passages, it is more like how one can imagine regretting a missed opportunity or regret injuring a friend's heart.

"...each man's work will become evident; for the day will show it, because it is to be revealed with fire; and the fire itself will test the quality of each man's work. If any man's work which he has built upon it remains, he shall receive a reward. If any man's work is burned up, he shall suffer loss; but he himself shall be saved, yet so as through fire."

—1 CORINTHIANS 13:13-15

Our choices in this life may bring us suffering in the loss of rewards, but even that suffering is set for a brief time.

"...for the Lamb who is in the midst of the throne will shepherd them and lead them to living fountains of waters. And God will wipe away every tear from their eyes."

—REVELATION 7:17

Scripture gives us confidence in approaching the Judgment or Bema Seat, and even hope and joy. Paul mentions often how he was motivated by future rewards at Christ's coming, rewards tied to the faithful brothers and sisters he was spurring on, and that his suffering was always held in light of that hope.

"For what is our hope, or joy, or crown of rejoicing? Is it not even you in the presence of our Lord Jesus Christ at His coming? For you are our glory and joy."

—1 THESSALONIANS 2:19-20

In an article on the doctrine of rewards, Pastor J. Hampton Keathley III, writes:

"Of course we should serve the Lord out of love and for God's glory, and understanding the nature of rewards will help us do that. But the fact still remains that the Bible promises us rewards. God gives us salvation. It is a gift through faith, but He rewards us for good works. God graciously supplies the means by which we may serve Him. Indeed, He works in us both to will and to do as we volitionally appropriate His grace...but the decision to serve, and the diligence employed in doing so, are our responsibility and our contribution and God sees this as rewardable."[54]

In our chapter on the irritant we talked about a splendor Lucifer once had. His splendor was lost through his arrogant choice to exalt himself above God. As believers in Jesus though, the splendor has been placed on us through grace. Our redemptive stories told and passed down have become God's splendor. As we embrace the labor of discerning them, of capturing them, of telling them to others, we regenerate the deep. We bring the redemptive hope of Christ with us to dark places in need of His light.

And we don't do it as martyrs. While we long for meaningful relationship with God and can have our full expectation on God to eagerly offer this to us as we trust Him in even little ways daily, we can also anticipate the joy of celebration with Him in Heaven. We want to obey God out of a place of love for His remarkable rescue and redemption of us, but we can also look forward to a mysterious but very real kind of treasure stored up on our behalf as we persevere in hard places. His grace has saved us, and His grace is giving us partnership in our eternal experience with Him that will be loaded with goodness without measure.

It's good friends, really good. The good news of Jesus is the best news we can get.

MY REDEMPTION STORY

The time came for me to make a decision. Jonathan and I were facing infertility, and for me it was the death of a dream and a brutal reminder that we are not Home yet. For some their awakening comes with a diagnosis, with a tragedy, with a closed door that will never open. We find ourselves in a crisis of faith where we can choose to drop out, drift, go the way of the prodigal child— still related, still forever secure, but wasting precious days in self-focus and meaningless activity. Or, we can choose to believe Jesus, believe He resurrects the dead and redeems the broken.

One afternoon on my living room floor, broken to the bone in grief, I chose the latter. I chose to pray our family prayer, that God would grow our family in quality and quantity but surrendered to His way of answering it. Within minutes of offering my belief, God gave me insight into His own heart. He showed me how it was a prayer of His that He had seeded in me, that He desired the growth of His own family in quality and quantity, and that I was made in His image and longed like He did for the same things. I began to remember verses and remembered too that the family of God is not grown through the procreation of physical bodies, but by regeneration through faith. It is the Gospel seed that bears life, and that is the seed I carried within me. I was fertile with the Gospel, and could be fruitful in my life, by God's grace.

The lie of infertility was that I could not create, that I was broken and had no life to offer. But just as God is the Creator and I was made in His image, that means I too am a creator-type. I create life with my words filled with His Word, with my redemptive stories, and with my life. Regardless of what my womb could do, my soul could bear life.

We were eventually blessed with the gift of parenting our daughter through the miracle of adoption and will forever be grateful for God's grace toward us in this way. We had hoped to adopt more children, but over time it seemed as if God was directing us in other ways. For almost a year we fostered a teen girl we hoped would heal with God's love in our home. Following that season we briefly expected twins through adoption, but that fell through at the last minute. When we went to resume our adoption journey to China, we learned about significant changes that led us to a decision to release that dream too. During the same week we were grieving these losses that came right after the other, my niece was born. We prayed for God to give us His peace and wisdom as we traveled to see her, but had no idea that God was about to make clear the path He was preparing for our family too.

While visiting my brother's family, Jonathan and I came to a peaceful decision to stop pursuing our family's growth through adoption. We had been through a lot in our parenting journey, and we believed we were just as God planned—the three of us. The morning after our decision, I woke one eye at a time, half expecting grief over the loss of a dream for more children. As I got up and poured my coffee, my brother asked me to come see what he bought his wife for her birthday. He had bought his wife plants that had he bought them for me would have been dead before we made it home. I swallowed down my coffee and tried to pay attention. But then he showed me his favorite plant.

According to plant folks, there is an attractive houseplant in the succulent family that grows tiny baby plantlets. These baby plantlets grow on the edges of the leaves, at every tip where she branches out. Eventually, they grow too heavy to be born any longer and simply drop to the surrounding soil, producing an altogether new plant of the same kind. It is often recommended that these plants be contained because of their invasive reproductive ways. If grown outdoors, you are warned to be prepared for she will take over the yard. A local nursery expert told my brother if he planted it in the backyard, "Good luck stopping her!" Why?

She is a mother of thousands.

And here is the kicker: a mother of thousands plants cannot produce seeds of their own.

She is barren, and yet she can launch a revolution.

The creative God of all things plant and person can bring revolution from the barren. Where we see an inability to bring life –whether it's through a broken soul or a broken womb, God sees the potential for generations seated at our tables in Heaven, filled with our forever families and children through faith. We do not grow God's family by procreation, but by regeneration through faith.

Later when I received the contract for this book, I was told it was best for me to start writing again on a blog. With much prayer and lots of unknown ahead, I launched out in faith with the blog, *A Mother of Thousands.* And I did it on my 40th birthday! From the womb of infertility heartache was born a hopeful vision of women—from teenagers to grandmothers—being released from shame so they can nurture generations of women in grace.

Now I don't know God's plans for me in this life. I don't know how long before I can stop praying *Maranatha*. I know though that I have been rescued. In many ways I have been comforted. I know that many wounded places in me have been transformed into lovely stories of hope I get to now share and use to comfort others. I don't cast my pearls before "swine", I don't grasp for every relationship and try to get everyone to listen and value my words or friendship. In our settings there will be people who will compete with us; they will be jealous of our voice or gifts or story and they will work against the will of God or will simply refuse to celebrate God's work in our lives. Best care practices for nourishing and displaying our redemptive stories, our pearls, include investing in intimate relationships wisely, and to root deep in the love and Word of God for our lives. Our culture celebrates big, noisy, high profile lives with all the "Likes" and "Followers" we can collect. I have learned the hard way to enter and build relationships open hearted, but with wisdom. What we carry is precious, it is the Gospel and it is life itself.

To all who have ears to hear, let them hear.

We can still get stuck singing old songs if we aren't prioritizing our soul's need for Sabbath. Recently I was speaking at a women's retreat and had some time with God to myself. It was a quiet retreat, so the purpose was to simply be with God in solitude and silence—so we can better see and hear what He may be wanting to say to us. I was tired and weary with all sorts of fears and failures I was secretly nursing, and I didn't know where to start with unloading my soul. A friend had just given me a little booklet of devotions prior to the quiet interlude, so I took it out and began to read. It only took a few lines before tears were pouring down my face, God was lifting my heart out of an old song I was stuck in that season and gave me a new song to sing before Him.

"You wail and bemoan your sin and failure before Me. Is this the song you bring? Is this what you would offer as praise before Me? Bring Me a song that revels in My wild and passionate love for you!

Tell Me child of My love—shall your wailing and crying that you are guilty glorify My love that has forgiven and wiped out your sin? Does your despair and depression at your creature weakness glorify Me when I have filled you with the strength of My fullness?

Have you forgotten that I have taken personal responsibility for you? Listen again if you have forgotten! I have made you My personal responsibility in becoming Man—becoming you and assuming all your indebtedness and judgment; I have made your history My history in order that you may participate in My life; that your weak humanity be filled with the fullness of who I am.

Behold the passion of My love. Look into its extremity that I should become you in order that you should become a participant in My love and a dance partner in My joy.

Let your imagination run riot with this wild purpose of My love!

Let this be the song you bring Me."[55]

We can forget that God has taken personal responsibility for us. We can forget the passion of His love for us. As we learn more about Jesus and grow in our relationship with Him we experience His sanctification work in us, a process where He refines us and separates us from our old nature forming us more and more like Christ.

"...you are in Christ Jesus, who became for us wisdom from God—and righteousness and sanctification and redemption—"

—1 CORINTHIANS 1:30

Sanctification is for the rest of our lives and is a painful process at times. We can grow weary and internalize the chiseling as God's displeasure—but this is farthest from the truth. C.S. Lewis describes this process of transformation in his book *Mere Christianity*:

> "The real Son of God is at your side. He is beginning to turn you into the same kind of thing as Himself. He is beginning, so to speak, to "inject" His kind of life and thought, His Zoe, into you; beginning to turn the tin soldier into a live man. The part of you that does not like it is the part that is still tin."[56]

There are days when all I feel is my tin not wanting to give way. Trials can wear us down and we can forget we have been given a new song to sing as we journey through this life. We can forget we are invited as a dance partner in God's joy. Sharing our stories with one another helps us remember to sing a new song.

When we capture and treasure our redemptive stories and pass them down to the next generation in our community, we are in a sense passing down our strands of pearls. We are saying, these were once buried symbols of affliction but now they are transformed works of art set on display that we want you to enjoy. Generations of women can be connected, though maybe having never met, because of the passing down of our unique strands of pearls—the stories of God's rescue and restoration work in the pain places of our lives.

We don't stay in hiding, afraid of what could happen to us as we step out and share. We don't let shame keep us from the deep, from connecting with women who could misunderstand us, judge us, belittle or betray us. We don't believe the lies that we are too small, too uneducated, too old, too heavy, too much, too little, or are from "the wrong side of town". We know we are not who we once were, and never can be, that we are new creations, with new names, new identities, and a new family. We return to relationships, we return to work, we return to creating, loving, sharing, inviting, giving, taking, eating, cleaning sinks of dishes, we return to sleep. We actively resist all the self-protective tendencies to isolate and retreat. It is a practice, a commitment to our own souls to live fully, to fulfill our purpose. Wisdom is our guide though, and we keep unlearning old ways as we learn new ways.

Just as little Wild Pearl filters her waters through her tiny hair-like gills, we are filtering messages in the cultural waters we swim in every day. Thousands upon thousands of thoughts fly by our minds, words and images flowing in and out, often without our conscious realization. It is inevitable then that we will take in something foreign and soon pollutants will work to cloud our minds. We learn to filter lies, we learn to capture them at the gills, in our thoughts. We practice taking in truth, over and over, so we recognize the taste of it and more easily detect what it is not. We practice the dip and swirl of the Sabbath, we pull away and refresh. But then we return. We bring with us regeneration. We bring with us Gospel, and by it alone we make the waters teem with life.

My husband and I buy old broken-down Chevy trucks of a certain model. A few years ago we bought one for me that was rusted and beaten down, scarred from neglect and erosion. Her coloring was silver and reminded me of pearl. There was a grit to her that drew me in and I had to buy her! As we negotiated her price I walked around her every edge admiring the way the light bounced off her bruises. She looked rough, like she had been run wild. I wondered where she had been, what she had seen, how she got the marks she wore. We made the deal and loaded her on a flatbed headed for a garage where we would rebuild her with fine detailed attention. I giggled as we followed behind her, I was delighting in the sight of her. Even though she was being hauled off helpless, I saw what she could become with my loving attention, so I named her my *Wild Pearl*. I could see her beauty even in her scars and right there was overcome by God's love for me in my own yet unfinished state. I cried as I considered this thought: if I could want a beat up old truck so much that I'd pay whatever was asked just to have her, even though she couldn't drive well and looked wretched, how much more did God want me?

When we reached the point of deciding what her exterior paint color would be I didn't hesitate. I wanted all her scarred places buffed so that they widened to let all the layers of color show through. They were nothing to be ashamed of because they told her story. I wanted her skillfully gutted and restored pristine in white on the inside, but just as she was on the outside, with a clear coat sealant.

I wanted her story to remind me of my story.

"They looked to Him and were radiant, and their faces were not ashamed."

—PSALM 34:5

No shame on our faces, indeed. Our beginnings are not our endings, God's story is moving on and our stories move on too. In the Gospel we find hope for turning our stories of shame into stories of splendor. And speaking of turning our stories around, let's return to Eve.

I believe God loved Eve. God did not endure her, blame her, or give her Adam's leftovers. God spoke as much through her design of His own nature as He did through Adam. In that moment when Adam could have chosen to obey God and resist the fruit Eve was chewing, leaving Eve condemned and alone in her sin, I wonder if God secretly fist-bumped His first-born for choosing to keep fellowship with her. I'm not saying Adam was right, it is always wrong to violate God's commands. I am just saying God knew how it was all going to go down, and God made a plan that worked to redeem Eve too.

And friend, He wants to redeem you.

May the hope of Wild Pearl, both the oyster and the truck, buoy us up in our moments of weakness. In our cry for *Maranatha* as a means of escape from our hard seasons, may we find strength and persevere. We will self-protect, we will cope poorly at times because we are human. We will build nacre around wounds and we will forget to believe Jesus. Even this though, God can redeem. Let us not lose heart, the story is about to finish, and the ending is going to be worth every step of the struggle.

Remember early on when I pointed out that there was no mention of the pearl in Eden? And why would there be? There was no affliction, no pain, and no need for repair. But at the end of the story in the book of Revelation we see the future kingdom for all those who are finally brought Home. We will enter glorious gates to an indescribable world because of our faith in Jesus. And friend, those gates will not be made of the exotic costly jewels or treasury of gold found in Eden. No, these gates will be made of something even more precious. God has reserved these gates of victory for His grand display of our little symbol of triumph: the pearl!

"The twelve gates were twelve pearls: each individual gate was of one pearl."

—REVELATION 21:21

Our hope is in the One savior, Jesus, who brings us one Gospel. And sure, had there been no woman, had there been no deception, had there been no sin, there would be no curse.

Oh, but there would be no pearl.

DISCUSSION QUESTIONS
12—THE SPLENDOR OF THE STORY

YOUR REDEMPTION STORY

God created you to enjoy you. How does this make you feel?

_____

_____

_____

God also made a way for you to enjoy redeeming what is broken in this world with Him. How does it feel to know you have a regenerating purpose in your world, in this generation?

_____

_____

_____

OTHER REDEMPTIVE STORIES

How are you tempted to forget that you have a regenerating purpose in your world today? What small stories do you tend to get stuck in that distract you from His story unfolding?

_____

_____

_____

What or who could you look to in your life to remind you of who you are and why you are here?

_____

_____

_____

your Display story

{Now you wrap it up! What a journey! Well done beautiful witnesses!}

Now that I am God's daughter by faith in Jesus, I know this is how God sees me:

_____

_____

Now I believe this about God:

_____

_____

I believe this about Jesus:

_____

_____

I believe this about the Holy Spirit:

_____

_____

I believe this about sin:

_____

_____

I believe this will happen to me after I die:

_____

_____

Now I can choose to respond to pain in my life by:

_____

_____

When I sin I know that:

_____

_____

With His power I can:

_____

_____

I am created with a unique personality, a unique setting, and a unique combination of talents and gifts, as well as spiritual gifts I can use to encourage others, such as:

_____

_____

your Pearl

Before I trusted in Christ I was separated from God because of sin in my heart. {Briefly add any other attributes you discovered in your Formation Story}

_____

_____

_____

_____

I believe Jesus lived, died and rose from the dead to cleanse me of my sins and save me. {Share when and where this event took place from your Retrieval Story}

_____

_____

_____

_____

As a daughter of God, sealed for eternity and filled with God's Spirit, I have a regenerating purpose in my world. I will fulfill the purposes He has specifically for me as I grow in my relationship with Him! {Briefly share one or a thousand of the ways you can imagine God using this—you Redemption story—and other redemptive stories to grow His family in quality and quantity!}

_____

_____

_____

_____

"You are the sweetest gift, my little pearl.
You are a bright young thing and the whole world
is in front of you.
Take things as they come and you will weather well.
Go everywhere.
Be brave and strong and free.
Keep your eyes and ears and heart wide open.
Look for goodness all around you.
And when you feel small in the great big world, be still.
Think of your beautiful roots.
They are deep and true and will allow you to stretch far.
So go into the world and let your little light shine.
And always remember you are loved and blessed
and the littlest one that ever stole my heart."
—REBECCA PUIG[57]

the Notes

INTRODUCTION

1   Chuck Swindoll, *Starting Over* (Originally published by Multnomah Press, 1977, now owned by Zondervan), pp. 40-41.

CH. 1 THE DEEP

2   "Celebration of Discipline" by Richard J. Foster. (San Francisco: Harper & Row, 1978), p. 1.

3   This fun fact about oysters came from the National Public Radio, Inc., blog called "the salt," in an article titled, "The Oyster's Mighty Comeback Is Creating Cleaner U.S. Waterways" found at https://www.npr.org/sections/thesalt/2016/07/31/488122810/the-oysters-mighty-comeback-is-creating-cleaner-u-s-waterways

4   1 Timothy 2:14

5   To read more on Marie Kondo's magical ways, and to see what I mean about the plight of the socks: "The Life-Changing Magic of Tidying Up," by Marie Kondo. (Ten Speed Press; 1st edition 2014), p.80-82.

6   These Bible teachings can be found at www.lesfeldick.org.

7   Written by yours truly.

CH. 2 THE CLUSTER

8   "Telling the Truth: The Gospel as Tragedy, Comedy, and Fairy Tale" by Frederick Buechner. (Harper & Row, 1977), p. 3.

9   See more about *The 700 Club* at www.cbn1.com.

10 For more information about how you can connect with Teen Challenge, see www.teenchallengeusa.com.

11 "Run Baby Run—The Explosive True Story of a Savage Street Fighter" by Nicky Cruz with Jamie Buckingham, with an Introduction by Billy Graham. (Bridge-Logos Publishers, 1988).

12 Thanks to contributing writer Cambria Bold at www.thekitchn. com for the insight into oyster's "gnarly shapes" in her article titled: "How Oysters Are Grown: A Visit to Island Creek Oysters in Duxbury, Massachusetts" that can be found here: https://www. thekitchn.com/island-creek-oysters-grower-tour-192689.

13 "Released from Shame—Moving Beyond the Pain of the Past" by Dr. Sandra Wilson. (IVP Press, 2002), p. 72.

CH. 3 THE IRRITANT

14 For more information about cultivating oysters, visit Go Deep Aqua Culture, and for more on their threats specifically, check out: http://godeepaquaculture.com/oysters/predators-and-threats/.

15 We are supremely blessed with excellent teaching pastors at Grace Fellowship Church in Johnson City, TN. Pastor Tom Oyler has been the senior pastor of our congregation since its inception, and in 2013 was awarded the first ever Alumni Distinguished Service Award by his alma mater, Dallas Theological Seminary.

16 Ezekiel 28:17

17 Exodus 20:16; 1 Peter 2:22; John 14:6, Romans 3:4; Numbers 23:19; 1 Samuel 15:29; John 17:17; Heb. 6:18; Isaiah 53:9.

18 Genesis 1:16 (NKJV). The word "made" comes from "asah" which means "to do or make", in contrast to verse 1 where God created out of nothing. The Hebrew word means, "to arrange or put in order" and scholars suggest God used materials already in existence from the prior creation. See for example, *Biblical Creation Truth*, by Joaozinho Da S. F. A. Martins, (Xulon Press, 2012), p. 396.

19 Ezekiel 28:7-8

20 "Battlefield of the Mind" by Joyce Meyer. (Warner Faith; Revised edition, 2002).

21 "The Screwtape Letters" by C.S. Lewis. (HarperOne; Reprint edition, 2015).

CH. 5 THE WOUND

22 Psalm 37:9

23 Hebrews 4:12

24 While this quote is often credited to C.S. Lewis because it pops up in the film *Voyage of the Dawn Treader* (2010), based on C.S. Lewis' book, this artful phrase was not written by him. But it sure does sound like something he would say! The praise goes instead to the brilliant screenwriters with clearly good taste: Christopher Markus, Stephen McFeely, and Michael Petroni.

25 Genesis 3:8b

26 Genesis 4:1

27 Genesis 6:11

28 "Released from Shame—Moving Beyond the Pain of the Past" by Dr. Sandra Wilson. (IVP Press, 2002), p. 24-27.

CH. 6 THE NACRE

29 Joel 2:12-13

30 Joel 2:26-27

31 Philippians 3:19

32 Genesis 4:25

33 "The Problem of Pain" by C.S. Lewis. (HarperOne; Revised ed. Edition, 2015).

34 "Emotionally Healthy Spirituality: Unleash a Revolution in Your Life in Christ", by Peter Scazzero. (Thomas Nelson, Inc., Reprint edition, 2011), p. 15.

35 "Mere Christianity" by C.S. Lewis. (HarperOne; Revised & Enlarged edition, 2015).

36 "Anatomy of the Soul; Surprising Connections between Neuroscience and Spiritual Practices That Can Transform Your Life and Relationships" by Dr. Curt Thompson. (Tyndale Momentum, June 1, 2010), p. 13.

37 Id. at 23.

38 Hosea 2:14

39 "The Four Loves" by C.S. Lewis. (HarperOne; Reissue edition, 2017).

CH. 8 THE OPENING

40 Ezekiel 36 depicts the old condition with the metaphor of a "heart of stone" replaced by God with a "heart of flesh". In Ephesians 4:18, Paul describes the old unregenerate state as having "hardness of heart" that is replaced. And in Ephesians 2:1-2, Paul describes our former life as when we were "dead in the trespasses and sins" in which we "once walked".

41 1 Corinthians 15:1-4

42 1 Peter 2:9-10

CH. 9 THE WASHING

43 A simple search of Google for "mother definition" offers this among other descriptions.

44 www.merriam-webster.com definition of *mother*.

45 Exodus 30:17-21

46 Steven Gertz was the editorial coordinator of *Christian History* magazine, a former publication of Christianity Today, © 2003. His article titled, "What is the pre-Christian history of the baptismal ceremony?" posted August 8, 2008, and can be found here: http://www.christianitytoday.com/history/2008/august/what-is-pre-christian-history-of-baptismal-ceremony.html. Used with permission.

47 Romans 6:4

CH. 10 THE SETTING

48 I am an Independent Ambassador for Noonday Collection. Noonday Collection's corporate mission statement and other information can be found here at www.mamabear.noondaycollection.com.

49 Is. 45:10-13; Rom. 9:20, 21

CH. 11 THE BEST CARE PRACTICES

50 "Gift From the Sea" by Anne Morrow Lindbergh. (Pantheon Books; 2nd edition, 1977).

51 See Pearls International's tips for properly caring for pearls at: https://pearlsinternational.com/the-biggest-mistake-pearl-people-make/

52 Worldwide English version.

53 For more information about Noonday Collection, see www.mamabear.noondaycollection.com.

CH. 12 THE SPLENDOR OF THE STORY

54 "The Doctrine of Rewards: The Judgment Seat (Bema) of Christ", written by J. Hampton Keathley III, Th.M.. Pastor Keathley was a 1966 graduate of Dallas Theological Seminary and a pastor for 28 years. See his full article available here: https://bible.org/article/doctrine-rewards-judgment-seat-bema-christ#P13_975

55 "From the Father's Heart" by Malcolm Smith, Devotional #3. Unconditional Love, International, see more at www.malcolmsmith.org.

56 "Mere Christianity" by C. S. Lewis. (HarperOne, an imprint of HarperCollins Publishers, 2001), p. 189.

57 This is a delightful quote that brought me to tears because I found it the day I finished writing my manuscript. It is perhaps more for me than any reader of these pages, but maybe God intends for you to enjoy its goodness too. It was written by Rebecca Puig, the founder of Sugarboo and Co., who told me she wrote it for her daughter. You can find it in a little book I purchased a year ago created by Sugarboo Designs out of Roswell, Georgia. The book is called, "The Little Book of Wisdom for Exquisite Ladies" which is altogether darling. As Rebecca says of herself—she is a "Dealer in Whimsy". I'm fairly certain you will agree. Find Rebecca at www.sugarbooandco.com.

FOR MORE RESOURCES
AND TO LEARN MORE ABOUT SHARING
YOUR STORY, VISIT US AT
WWW.ALLTHEWILDPEARLS.COM